MORE
GREAT
RAILWAY
JOURNEYS

MORE GREAT RAILWAY JOURNEYS

BENEDICT ALLEN

CHRIS BONINGTON

HENRY LOUIS GATES JR

BUCK HENRY

BEN OKRI

ALEXEI SAYLE

VICTORIA WOOD

WITH COMMISSIONED PHOTOGRAPHS BY
TOM OWEN EDMUNDS
AND DUNCAN WILLETS

BBC BOOKS

FRONTISPIECE View from the train driver's window approaching Thurso, Scotland

This book is published to accompany the television series
More Great Railway Journeys first broadcast in 1996.
Executive Producer: David Taylor
Rachael Heaton-Armstrong was Assistant Producer on the programme *London to Arkadia*

ISBN 0 563 38717 3

Designed by Andrew Shoolbred

First published in 1996 by BBC Books,
an imprint of BBC Worldwide Publishing.
BBC Worldwide Limited, Woodlands, 80 Wood Lane, London W12 0TT.

Set in Berling by Ace Filmsetting Ltd., Frome
Colour separations by Radstock Reproductions Ltd., Midsomer Norton
Printed in Great Britain by Cambus Litho Ltd., East Kilbride
Bound in Great Britain by Hunter and Foulis Ltd., Edinburgh
Jacket by Lawrence Allen Ltd., Weston-super-Mare

Contents

Aleppo to Aqaba

ALEXEI SAYLE

T HE MOST FAMOUS TRAIN JOURNEY in the world, the one that everyone has
heard of, was the old Orient Express; yet how many people know
where that journey ended? The answer is in the Syrian city of Aleppo,
and it was from this terminus of one great rail journey that I hoped to start
another – one that would eventually take me by rail to the Red Sea port of
Aqaba. The centrepiece of my proposed journey would be the Hejaz Railway,
a relic of the days of the Ottoman Empire which ran from Damascus to
Medina. Begun in 1907 but never completed, the Hejaz was all but crippled
by 1917. It had one of the shortest lifespans of any railway in the world, yet
in its way it is as famous as the Orient Express. Most people have probably not
heard of its name – the Hejaz – but I am sure that most people will be aware
of it as the railway line that was repeatedly blown up by Lawrence of Arabia.
My journey would find out what was left of this short-lived line.

I came to make this journey partly because I am a sceptic. When people
who do travel programmes on the television are interviewed they often say
things like: 'Yes, I know it looks like we're having an expenses-paid holiday,
but it's not like that at all. It's jolly hard work.' If you're a cynic like me you
think, 'Yeah, sure, it looks like an all-expenses paid holiday, because that's just

Alexei Sayle sets off in style on one of the most romantic train journeys in the world

what it is.' So when the BBC asked me to film an episode of their new series *Great Railway Journeys of the World* I leaped at the chance, particularly when the journey I was offered was this rail trip in the Middle East. Who wouldn't relish the prospect of wandering south through Syria and Jordan, visiting en route such wonders of the world as the great Crusader fort of Krak des Chevaliers and Petra, the rose-red city half as old as time? Sounded like a holiday tailor-made for me.

However, it was not long into the journey before the terrible truth dawned – all those travel journalists were telling the truth! You have to get up really, really early and work all day. Because you're making a film you stand with your back to all the sights. The second you've finished filming, you're packed into a car and driven somewhere else with no time to wander around. You stand in the heat and say the same thing over and over again, and retrace your steps time and time again until it's photographed just how the cameraman wants. In the evening you fall instantly asleep at the dinner table with your head in the kebabs.

Luckily I didn't know all this when I set off. I couldn't sleep with excitement beforehand, and lay awake pondering what I had that I could uniquely bring to this film. I'm the type of Westerner who thinks they have a special affinity for the Arab world and I somehow feel at home there. Sayle of Arabia, perhaps. Things that would drive me screaming mad in Africa make me smile with tolerant affection when done by Arabs. But my Arab friends in England are all very educated, urban, cosmopolitan types and my time in the Middle East has been very limited to date, so I wonder if this indulgent affection will withstand the test of an extended trip in difficult circumstances meeting the equivalent of the man on the Clapham omnibus – the man on the Jericho camel, perhaps.

To prepare for this journey, because I was visiting an area that is both the cradle of our civilization and a contemporary hot-spot of gigantic geopolitical significance, I of course spent most of my time thinking about what I was going to wear on camera. Finally I decided on a lightweight tropical gabardine suit in a sort of stone colour, a three-button grey Gap top, some very nice suede walking boots from K Shoes and, literally to top the whole ensemble off, a jaunty canvas hat with just the cutest turned-up brim – rather like what you might see a trained bear on a trike in a circus wearing (except you wouldn't go and see anything so barbaric, I hope). This hat was one of four in different colours that I'd bought in Mallorca, and on the front was embroidered in multi-coloured cotton 'Mallorca Island of Dreams' – they seemed perfect for this trip. I took two of these hats with me, but things started going wrong before I'd even left England and they got left at the Royal Jordanian check-in desk at Heathrow. So I arrived hatless in Gaza – or near there anyway. Frantic phone calls to England resulted in my two spare hats and the original hats (which had turned up at lost property) all being express parcelled to arrive the next day in Damascus. Except they didn't. You see, DHL, Fed-Ex and the rest don't operate in Syria – you have to use a local company instead. The result was the next we heard of the hats they were in Dubai and were planning to stay there for a while as the next day was a Friday (the Arab Sabbath) and the day after that was Islamic New Year's Day. While they were in Dubai, my hats saw all the major tourist attractions: they went on a jeep safari to Wadi Hatta and took a half-day excursion to the Jemeira Mosque. I told the hats to meet me in Damascus. They went to Aleppo and spent an action-packed few days staying at the historic Baron Hotel and visiting the world-renowned Citadel. We finally all met up in Amman, Jordan. The peregrinations of my hats rather distracted me for the first few days of the trip, which was probably just as well as it consisted largely of sitting in airports at ungodly hours of the day and night with not a train in sight, before we finally arrived at the starting-point of our trip proper.

I realized as soon as the trip proper started that I shouldn't have come on it. Before I left I thought: 'It'll be great. I'll take lots of interesting, primitive trains. I'll chat to lots of interesting foreigners. I'll have to be independent, thrown back on my inner resources.' As soon as I landed at Damascus Airport I realized that (1) I don't like primitive trains, (2) I hate talking to foreigners and (3) I have no inner resources. I'm always doing this. I must think I'm someone else. I don't know who this bloke is, the one who wants to be a rufty-tufty explorer type. He's certainly not me.

OVERLEAF **Successive invasions and a major earthquake have not destroyed the magnificence of the moated citadel which dominates the city of Aleppo**

Actually I think I did find the other bloke who's always getting me into trouble. I found him in the departure hall of Damascus Airport. Before we could begin our rail journey we had to fly into Damascus and then connect with a plane to Aleppo. Me and the BBC film crew had to get up at 3 a.m. My first reaction when I heard our call time was, 'You mean there's a three o'clock in the morning as well?' An hour later and we still hadn't got to customs with our tons of silver boxes, containing all our filming equipment, plus nobody had any idea when our plane would take off. Now, as far as I can recall I've never been up and about at 4 a.m. in my life before, but at this time of the morning I seem to be a totally different person. I went to get everybody coffee from a little snack bar I found open, I helped carry some of the lighter gear on and off the X-ray machines, and I kept everybody's spirits up by reciting comic Victorian music hall monologues. The film crew were gob-smacked, wondering where the surly, miserable, unhelpful, whiny git that they usually had to put up with had got to. So that must be it. Between, say, about 4 a.m. and 6.45 a.m. I'm the bloke who'd like to be an explorer. In my sleep I'm a friendly, open, well-adjusted fellow you'd be happy to entrust your life to. If I was videotaped in my sleep it would probably show me smiling, nodding, muttering witty aphorisms and translating Plutarch from the original Latin. Unless you come round to my house in the middle of the night, you'll never meet this chap.

The real trip started in Aleppo, little known to us Westerners but once one of the Orient's greatest cities. It claims to be the oldest inhabited city in the world. I know other cities such as Amman and Milton Keynes also claim this, but Aleppo does have a pretty strong claim. And now, thanks to currency restrictions, it also has some of the oldest inhabited cars in the world. Everywhere you go you are nearly run over by old Chevrolets, Austins, Peugeots and Studebakers. It's a privilege to be injured by some of them. Aleppo was the confluence of the two great caravan routes to the West – the Silk Road and the Spice Road. It has always been a melting pot of Kurds, Armenians, Christians, Jews and Arabs, brought together literally under one roof – the great souk or market which covers over 20000 square metres of Aleppo's crowded city streets. All this and more brought the Orient Express to its terminus here, so it seemed a good place for my journey to begin.

We stayed in the Baron Hotel, once world-famous as it was built to house travellers on the Orient Express, but now most kindly described as having faded somewhat. The pride and joy of its owner, Sally Mazioumian, is its battered guest book which reads like a *Who's Who* of the early twentieth century: T. E. Lawrence of course (no getting away from him round here), Agatha Christie (who wrote *Murder on the Orient Express* at the hotel while her husband was excavating the dead cities that surround Aleppo), Theodore Roosevelt, Charles Lindbergh and so on and on. They are all in there plus a whole load of people you've never heard of but who were real big shots in their day. 'That's Count Ostrowsky,' Sally would say, 'the famous canoeing balloonist', or 'That's Tommy Shinbone. Nobody's heard of him now, but in his day he was terribly, terribly famous as radio's first comedy gynaecologist. He arrived here with Ted Ray and Max Ernst in his own airship from Beirut, and such a crowd gathered that he had to be carried to the hotel in a bucket.'

It's the phrase 'Nobody's heard of him now' that gives me the total heebie-jeebies about guest books, conjuring up a vision of Ozymandias's legs standing all alone in the desert with nothing left of all his mighty works, his human vanities and vast accomplishments but sand. People like Tommy Shinbone, hugely celebrated in their era, but now dead, forgotten, all their achievements, all their pride reduced to a scratchy signature in a tattered old book. It's enough to give a less stable person than me a panic attack – aaargh, I can't breathe, I can't breathe, is that the floor coming up to meet me, Sooty? Thunk. Silence. (Act II. Alexei's room, later that same morning. He climbs off the floor and continues writing.) I didn't tell Sally Mazioumian any of this, of course – she'd think I was nuts.

The journey began with a train to the Mediterranean city of Lattakia. This line is one of the newest in the Middle East, completely rebuilt by the Syrians a few years ago with assistance from East Germany and the Soviet Union. It is one of the greatest railway engineering masterpieces of the world, yet no one outside Syria seems to have heard of it. The train started out across an agricultural plain and after an hour or so approached what seemed to be a

OVERLEAF **Aleppo's vast souk is a microcosm of the Middle East, where Arab, Christian and Jewish shopkeepers sell spices, carpets, beaten copper vessels and much more**

solid mountainous wall. Somehow it threaded its way through an unseen gap and then launched into a high-wire act, viaducts and tunnels following in quick succession as we passed through spectacular valleys and mountain ridges. Switzerland, eat your heart out! We in the West have a clichéd view of the Middle East as a land of barren desserts, religious fanatics and perpetual wars, so it's good to be brought up short and made to reconsider our prejudiced views.

Lattakia was another surprise for me. The city (which I must admit I'd never heard of before I visited it) is modern, bleached white with an upbeat feel. The women mostly dress with a recognizably Mediterranean exuberance – very few of them are wrapped in Muslim shrouds. I almost feel I could be in Greece or Turkey, except that my belongings are a lot safer here. That's one of the good points of this region that nobody seems to mention – you can leave your luggage unattended for hours, safe in the knowledge that it will still be waiting for you when you come back. And the people are so hospitable and friendly – which is all the more commendable in Syria because it is a police state. Everywhere you go in this country you see uniforms and guns. The military make up the police force, and military service is compulsory. Jobs have to be found for all these men, so almost everything is under armed guard. On top of this, Syria has several feared internal intelligence organizations.

Apart from all my other problems I suffer from mild paranoia – I don't like to go to rugby matches because when the players go into a scrum I think they're all talking about me. But for the first time in my life I really was being followed everywhere by swarthy, thuggish men, my phone really was being tapped, and everywhere I went I needed papers of permission from sinister ministries housed in frightening faceless concrete Lubyankas. Believe me, this state of affairs works wonders as a short-cut to total insanity.

Syria also has one of the last remaining old-style personality cults. Everywhere you go there are posters, statues and wall paintings of President Hafez Al-Assad, who came to power in 1970 in a bloodless coup. I wonder if when Assad is being driven through the streets of Damascus he thinks, 'Oooh, look, there's a big photo of me . . . oooh, look, there I am again and . . . who's that big statue of? Why, gee-willikers, it's me!' This Big Brother omnipresence is supposed to induce an effect of thorough intimidation and I'm sure it works on the average Syrian – indeed, one man I interviewed tried to tell me that the weather was much better under Assad than it had been under previous administrations – but as I was only temporarily subject to the capricious whims of his security police all this hagiography had a different effect on me. For a start, old Hafez doesn't look like the cruel tyrant he undoubtedly is; his photos failed to conjure up in me that chilling Orwellian image of the future of a boot stamping on a human face – for ever. Rather, he resembles some slightly seedy Levantine lounge act, so that the posters plastered everywhere give the impression that this geezer with the toothbrush moustache and comb-over is in town to give a concert, something like 'Ahmed Tabouleh and his Bazouki Music of the Mountains' at the Sheraton Hotel Oasis Rooms, and the tickets have been selling really slowly so the concert promoter has been forced to stick up posters everywhere in a desperate attempt to drum up some interest.

From Lattakia I travelled to Hama, stopping en route at one of the greatest surviving monuments to past holy wars – Krak des Chevaliers, the largest and most intact of all the Crusader castles. Physical reminders of wars past are everywhere, and at Krak I was reminded of one of the other effects still troubling the Middle East – the displacement of people from the homes their families have lived in for centuries. My guide to the castle was a man called Whaled Mourad; with him was his father, who was born within the walls of the castle where the original village of Krak was established. Until 1936 this was home to ten thousand people; then the French, who had had a colonial mandate over Syria since 1920, decided they wanted to restore the place as a tourist attraction and threw them all out. Many of the inhabitants had to emigrate; those who remained built the present-day village that now stands in the shadow of the castle. It's a poignant sight repeated all over the region – the Palestinian standing on the Jordanian side of the River Jordan pointing across to where his parents, grandparents and ancestors had lived for hundreds of years and where now he and his children are not allowed to set foot.

As late evening fell we arrived in nearby Hama, famous for its *norias*. These are thirteen giant wooden water-wheels which have turned without interruption for more than six centuries, diverting water from the River Orontes into narrow aqueducts high above the pathways. All the wheels groan

ABOVE The white-gloved guard of the train to Hama

OPPOSITE A fellow passenger to Hama, wearing traditional Syrian dress

on their ancient axles, letting out a noise that seems to have been dragged out of their distant past. There was something else quite striking about Hama which I took in only subconsciously at first – there were hardly any pictures of President Assad. I later found out that the reason has to do with an attempt by the Muslim Brotherhood to take over the city in 1982. The revolt was ruthlessly crushed by Assad, and the death toll may have been as high as thirty thousand. Today the city is still a traditional Muslim stronghold, and hearing of the relatively recent bloody fighting gave the groaning of the water-wheels added significance. Syria's people seem so universally pleasant that it's hard to work out why their rulers have to sit on them so hard. But then it's easy to forget that Syria has been at war with Israel for decades. Denying basic civil rights in the name of this war has suited Israeli and Arab tyrants alike.

We'd arrived in Syria at Damascus Airport, but had not yet visited the city proper. Now our train pulled in there. It was rather a disappointment at first, as we arrived in a scruffy suburb at the less than glamorous station of Cadam. But Cadam had its secrets – just across the tracks behind a broken line of old wagons lay the relics of one of the great railway lines of the twentieth century. Built by the Turks – ostensibly to transport pilgrims to Mecca but in reality to make tax-collecting easier across the vast Ottoman Empire – the Hejaz Railway is better known for its destruction than for its construction. When T. E. Lawrence needed something to unite the Arabs in revolt against their Turkish masters during World War I, the railway provided an inviting target. There in Cadam stand rotting rows of steam engines once run by anxious drivers wondering whether the next culvert would contain enough dynamite to lift their train into the nearest sand dune. In the nearby weeds stands the imperial dining coach of the Sultan of Turkey. Oh, God, this is like the guest book of the Baron Hotel all over again; I can feel the futility of human endeavour overwhelming me. Only one thing for it – I'll go shopping.

I headed straight for a Street called Straight which is now part of the famous Damascus souk. Now one of the really annoying things about the Arab world is that you can't just go and buy something – you have to haggle for it. You can't just say, 'How much is that, mate?' He says, 'A pound.' You give him the pound and you take whatever it is. No. You have to spend six hours insulting each other's trousers and family and drinking super-sweet mint tea and tasting goat on a stick, and when you buy the bloody thing it's still a pound. And let's face it – when have you ever bought anything you ever wanted, let alone needed, while you were on holiday? Yes, that's one of the secrets of the seasoned traveller – buying something for practically nothing that I don't want and is just too big for my suitcase.

A trip to the Hejaz Railway terminal in the centre of Damascus threatened a return of my existential angst. It stands in isolation, marooned by the city's endless traffic jams. The only hope you have of crossing to the booking hall is to wait for the cars to gridlock noisily and then skip through the tiny gaps left between the bumpers. The station itself is magnificent, an elaborate turn-of-the-century Ottoman building. On one of the walls is a faded, peeling timetable headed 'Palestine Railways 1922'. The timetable holds out the promise of an extraordinary 520-mile journey from Damascus to Cairo in little over twenty-four hours, travelling in comfort on the night sleeper, eating on starched tablecloths and watching some of the world's most spectacular scenery go by. The train would have gone around the Lebanon and Golan hills, passing through Haifa, Jerusalem and Gaza, and crossing the Sinai Desert and the Suez Canal. What a trip it must have been – but the last through train ran nearly fifty years ago. Palestine Railways disappeared in 1948 when the state of Israel was created and the first Arab–Israeli war severed the connections. There is now talk of repairing the Damascus–Cairo track. The disconnected railway line is a metaphor for the area's severed links, and its restoration would be wonderful proof of a new harmony and peace in the region. For now it's a journey I can just dream about – I had to press on with the one in hand. Once in the beautifully decorated booking hall, buying a ticket is simple enough. A full-time staff at the station attends to your needs and questions and you pass straight through to the platforms where you find that no trains run from the station – for that it's back to Cadam. It's like a variation on the old joke of the doors being open, the lights on, but nobody's home – hey, mister, your railway station's got no trains.

At Cadam we picked up the ironically named International Train to Amman in Jordan. This train leaves once a week, and if I wasn't travelling on it I'd think it was a joke. While you probably know that the Great Western Railway in Britain was designed and built by the engineer Brunel, I reckon that

ABOVE The engine workshops at Cadam in the suburbs of Damascus

OPPOSITE A relic of a more splendid age: antique Hejaz Railway rolling stock from the
days of the Ottoman Empire

23

Syrian Railways were designed and built by the Spanish surrealist Buñuel. This is the only explanation I can think of for the so-called International Train. It's a collection of ex-Budapest Metro carriages with their doors jammed permanently open, as are the windows, to let the dust in. It's pulled by an old Romanian diesel. Most of the passengers are Syrian secret policemen and it takes ten hours to complete a 200-mile trip, jolting over narrow-gauge track that hasn't been replaced since the Turks laid it. The diesel loco seems to come close to finding its own route off the rails as it twists and screams round tight curves. The train passes several Hejaz stations that are little more than ruins. There are no such luxuries as a buffet or even working toilets on board. Practically no one is on board. Especially not foreigners. The bus trip to Amman is much quicker, more comfortable and cheaper. Only a fool or a secret policeman would make the journey by train.

So why does the train run at all? The answer probably goes back to the origins of the line, whose religious foundations persist to this day. The line is held in trust – a *Waqf* – between Syria, Jordan and Saudi Arabia – though Saudi has little track and what there is disappears into the nearest sand dune. This trust, whose members never meet, is supposed to be responsible for the upkeep of the railway – something which the Syrians obviously take with a pinch of salt. I can only surmise that the Damascus-to-Amman service is kept alive by the Syrians in case this toehold into two other countries ever comes in handy. Few Syrians know of its existence and nobody knows when the trains are supposed to leave. It's a very Arab railway, which reminds me of Syria itself. Syria is a country that manages to combine the Arab love of prompt time-keeping, unemotional behaviour and a tireless work ethic with the well-known benefits of old Soviet-style state socialism. It's a sort of East Germany with hummus. You try and figure it out (and you have plenty of time to ponder on this trip), but any number of possible explanations don't quite add up. Though I can't quite figure out what keeps the Hejaz Railway running, in a way – a masochistic sort of way – I'm glad it does.

Five bone-shattering hours later we actually arrived at the border town of Dera'a where the Syrian diesel is replaced by a smart Jordanian Railways American diesel, hitched to the beaten-up carriages of the International Express. While this engine change took place I went for a walk round Dera'a.

Now, I seem to remember that something happened here – between Lawrence and a Turkish officer, if my memory is correct. I'll just look it up in my guidebook. Dera'a, Dera'a . . . here we are. Ooh, blimey. I have to say in all fairness that no one really knows for sure what happened to Lawrence so I decided to give the town the benefit of the doubt, but I went straight back to the station at a smartish clip anyway.

We actually made a 25-mile detour from Dera'a to the Roman city of Bosra where a music and arts festival is held in the Roman amphitheatre. As you pull into Bosra the scene is dominated by the massive Arab fort which encases the old amphitheatre. I liked Bosra very much – it was not the usual sterile monument, but a living city. People have made their homes among the remains of the Roman and Nabatean city and you see some amazing structures. The houses are fairly dull breeze-block affairs but some incorporate antique structures, so you might find one corner of a banal house is made up of a magnificent Roman column. There is of course a fly in the ointment, one we encountered several times – there is now talk of ejecting the inhabitants and 'cleaning the place up' for tourists. I think it would be a pity if this happened because one gets a wonderful sense of the continuity of history there now.

We rejoined the international express to continue our journey proper. As the train crossed the border from Syria to Jordan it seemed to cross a cultural divide. First impressions were of a more prosperous, relaxed and open country. Where Syria resembled a building site with half the houses seeming either derelict or left half-finished, northern Jordan was full of neat, pretty trackside villages. The atmosphere on the train changed too. The officious, suspicious Syrian border police were still on board – they stayed until Amman – but they suffered a loss of authority as the friendlier Jordanian security guards moved in. These Jordanian police actually smiled and were capable of uttering the phrase 'Welcome' without the implied sub-text from the Syrian guards which completes the greeting as 'you Zionist lackey'. Typically for me, no sooner was I out of Syria than I started to miss it. For all the awfulness of the regime, the people were some of the most welcoming I've ever met and were amazingly patient with me.

As we hit the outskirts of Amman we came across a strange piece of young Arab machismo. The rules are that you have to walk on the tracks straight at the train until it gets really close to you. This means that the train actually slows to a crawl and has to sound its horn constantly. Now there's one big difference between Syria and Jordan. Syria is full of Syrians. Jordan is full of Palestinians. A recent census showed that over 70 per cent of Jordan's population has Palestinian roots. One of them is Abdullah Toukan, an old friend of mine from student days in Liverpool. Nobody's ever done a survey on this, but I'm convinced that nearly everyone who's been to university in Britain will have known someone of world prominence who was just a humble student with them. My wife went to Bangor University at the same time as a bloke who went home to Mauritius to become leader of the opposition and later Prime Minister. For me it was Abdullah – he's now head of the Royal Jordanian Air Force and a negotiator with the Israelis on the details of the Peace Accord. So, anyone reading this who's still a student, be nice to that overseas student down the hall, that Paul or Wasim or Kwame, or he might come back and bomb your house. I met Abdullah at his aunt's house up in the royal compound on a hill outside Amman. It was good to see him and have one of those enjoyable conversations catching up with news of old friends, and very good to hear his optimism about the new mood of peace and rapprochement in the area. He is working near the centre of the political activity to bring the different factions closer together and it was most encouraging to hear, from a position of such authority, how upbeat he felt about the future of the region.

Back at Amman Station I travelled south on a steam engine driven by Fatallah, the last steam engine driver of the last working steam train in Jordan. Although the original Hejaz line ran all the way to Medina in what is now Saudi Arabia, the only passenger services south of Amman these days are for the benefit of tourist groups: today Fatallah is hauling a load of Austrian bankers on a fun excursion to Jiza, just over 20 miles away. As the train pulls off I can't help thinking this is a strange chemistry – Teutonic money-changers, me wondering whether I should tell them I'm Jewish and all of us being entertained by Palestinians. The steam train has a long hard pull up to the desert plateau above the city. As it does so it passes through what must be the largest refugee city in the world. Many of the Palestinians who live in this and similar camps elsewhere in Jordan were born there and have known no other home. The train passes just a few metres from the shanty houses, allowing us

An area of the train graveyard at Cadam

a glimpse of their dreadful physical conditions. I know the Austrians are along just for entertainment and, seemingly oblivious of the poverty surrounding them, they wave good-naturedly at the refugees as the train passes through. Once in the desert the organizers of our trip have arranged for the Austrians to be attacked by genuine Bedouins and their women carried (briefly) off. The tourists seem not to notice, much less to care, that they're being cast as the bad guys, the Turks, in a kitsch retread of Lawrence of Arabia. This is Arabia as they'd imagined it. This is what tourism seems to amount to all over the world – reducing everything to a sort of sanitized theme-park experience.

Leaving the tourists behind, I continued southwards with Fatallah's train all to myself for a while. He was taking me to join a train that takes phosphate from the open-cast desert mines down to Jordan's only port at Aqaba. The train runs through the Jordanian desert in a part of the world that Lawrence would have known well. It's here and southwards that he concentrated on bringing trains off the tracks – which by some strange coincidence is exactly what happened to us. At a small station just south of Jiza our train came off the rails and toppled sideways with a crash. This time it wasn't dynamite but the sheer antiquity of the track that caused the derailment; the cast-iron track dates back to the turn of the century and is basically worn out. It took a fair amount of BBC wheeling and dealing to get me another ride to join my phosphate train. Although on this trip I went first on a specially hired train and then on a freight train, it may not be long before the track is upgraded and passenger trains start to run along it again because the line runs past two of the most spectacular sites in the world, let alone the Middle East: Petra and Wadi Rum.

The approach to Petra is breathtaking. The entire city was chiselled into the walls of the Great Rift Valley by the pre-Roman Nabateans. You approach through what used to be the only way in and out of the city – a half-mile-long crack in the mountain known as the Siq. You twist and turn through the Siq until suddenly there in front of you is the marvellous Treasury building. Depending on the time of day, the rock which the buildings are carved from can glow pink or red or purple. The city is vast, all carved out of the solid rock. I climbed high up above it, past the sacrificial arena known as the High Place to what many regard as the finest of all Petra's structures, the Monastery. The tourists have not yet managed to spoil the totally beguiling experience that is Petra, though it may not be long before they intrude as Petra is one of the dubious beneficiaries of both the Peace Treaty and the end of the Gulf War. Before, it used to be a difficult trip to get to Petra; now, it can be a day out from the Israeli resort of Eilat.

Refreshed in spirit from the beauty of Petra, I got to make the least comfortable part of my journey – in the spare cab of the phosphate train. Two enormous diesels were linked together on this train not so much for pulling power as for stopping power – it was downhill all the way now from the desert plateau to the sea. Along the way we passed Bat na Ghoul or Belly of a Devil. Heaven knows why it's called that, but it's the place where the original Hejaz Railway line veers sharp left and heads for Medina, though it does not reach it, petering out as soon as it reaches the border of Saudi Arabia. We went straight ahead for Wadi Rum. It's here that Lawrence mania really reaches its peak because this was not only the base from which the Arab Revolt launched its attack on Aqaba, it was also the location for much of the shooting of David

Lean's movie *Lawrence of Arabia*. It is a spectacularly beautiful valley between vertiginous mountains and with a deep, sandy desert floor. Here again, those who have known the region for a long time are ambivalent about the increased tourism that the Peace Treaty has brought. It you want tranquillity and solitude now you'll have to share it with a few dozen others. Lawrence has a lot to answer for.

The rest of the journey down to Aqaba was much more prosaic – not the romantic vast emptiness of Wadi Rum, but scrubby waste resembling a huge building site. Then we passed a giant lorry park and suddenly we were at journey's end – Aqaba. I felt amazed I'd managed to make the journey by train. It's astonishing that the railways are still here at all. Battered by a century of war and upheaval they still somehow hang on, a tenuous thread that is a kind of symbol of hope among all the chaos and suffering that the Middle East has had to endure. It is also in Aqaba that you get a real sense of the explosive intimacy of the Middle East: on the far shore was the Egyptian Sinai Desert; below me was the Jordanian port of Aqaba and to the left, sharing the same beach, was Eilat in Israel. Aqaba is a meeting-place of clashing cultures and religions. But it's also a place where, hopefully, a happier future for the Middle East is being mapped out. Until recently the cheek-by-jowl resorts of Eilat and Aqaba could have been thousands of miles apart as there was no way of crossing between the two, but now there is a new crossing-point for tourists, bringing closer the Israeli dream of a Red Sea Riviera. To this end the Israelis are building a 'Peace Promenade' which runs along the coast from the Jordanian border near Aqaba to its frontier with Egypt. So there is a real spirit of optimism in the air here. But for me one of the things I feared had happened: me and the Arab world had been on holiday together for three weeks and we didn't like each other as much as we did before. For every good thing I'd found, I'd found a bad thing. Astonishing personal honesty, but appalling bureaucratic obstinacy; a real sense of culture and history, and a casual disregard for this culture and history; tremendous hospitality, and tremendous cruelty to animals. I think I'm going to have to find another continent to patronize. Sayle of Greenland, perhaps.

Mombasa to the Mountains of the Moon

BENEDICT ALLEN

T HE MOUNTAINS OF THE MOON had seemed to me as a child like the end of a rainbow – somewhere beyond reach, a hidden place of dreams and wonder. But even as a ten-year-old boy I knew that this faraway sleeping giant, something moulded from the soul of Africa, must have worked its magic on others before me.

The mountains first formally made themselves known to the outside world through the maps of Ptolemy, the Egyptian father of modern geography. In AD 150 he marked them down as the source of the great River Nile – itself something of a mystery, and said by some to be the 'four fountains' mentioned by the Greek historian Herodotus six hundred years earlier. The mountains became something of a Holy Grail for the Victorians, who sought them out for decades before they finally unravelled the geography of the African interior in their search for the Nile's source. And now I had arrived in Mombasa on the Kenyan shore of the Indian Ocean, and the Mountains of the Moon, today known as the Ruwenzoris, lay only a railway ride inland. Some of their peaks reached 5000 metres, capped by snow and banked by glaciers. They were out there waiting for me, just 800 miles through Kenya, beyond Lake Victoria and across Uganda towards Zaire. All I had to do was follow the line.

Benedict Allen on the footplate of an old steam locomotive in the Rail Museum in Nairobi

The city of Mombasa may be clogged with traffic nowadays, but it still echoes with the mixed Arab-African heritage of the coastal Swahili – all the vibrancy of equatorial Africa, interwoven with strands of Islam. And on my last visit, three years ago, I'd also noted that the economy apparently depended on dubious nightclubs full of aid workers and UN soldiers busily recuperating between stints in the neighbouring war zones. Meanwhile, the port down the road was thriving from the spoils of the very same wars. Mombasa seemed a parasite, thriving off Africa's misfortunes. It fed off the amoral earnings of passing strangers.

Of course I was being unfair; but returning now to the old port, I found I hadn't been quite as unfair as I'd thought. Loot was being unloaded from war-riven Somalia – sack after sack of telephone wiring and roof tiles. The stevedores were toiling away like termites, just as they always had: silently, unquestioningly, unloading for the Arabs, the Portuguese and the local Swahili – whoever then held the city. For over four centuries the powers fought back and forth for control of the coast's lucrative trade with India and the Far East. They left behind the tooled wooden doorways of Omani dynasties, crumbling colonial masonry, a reeking port-side fish market. But these things, and things like henna-adorned hands – all that makes up old Mombasa – also owe their origins to the slave trade, the Arab traffic in African flesh.

It's always easier to digest an alien culture at village level, so a Swahili friend took me off to a mud and wattle settlement on the outskirts of the city. It was a coconut palm place of wandering chickens, roaming goats, and running, screaming children with bright white teeth who gleefully called out to me the only English they knew: 'How are you? How are *yoooou?*' The local *mganga*, or healer, looked the least promising healer I think I've ever met – and I've met tribal healers you wouldn't let loose on your pet parrot. Dressed in a stained shirt with a hospital name tag that pronounced he was 'Dr Hamisi', he didn't seem to be able to walk in a straight line. He burped as he talked, incoherently, about his miraculous cures. It was just the level of professionalism that has always given witchdoctors a bad name.

When I returned with the film crew to see him in action he was more impressive, not even allowing the cameraman a second take. The Swahili traditionally believe that when someone is sick it's because a spirit has entered the body. The *mganga*'s job is to identify the spirit's personality – mischievous, or downright evil – and then draw it out with entrancing music. 'Dr Hamisi' sat himself down importantly in the dust near a cashew tree, three assistants with drums arranging themselves equally importantly behind. As the villagers gathered to see the spectacle, the *mganga* spread out his tools of trade – gnarled bones, the crumbling bark of obscure trees, a goat's horn and a tray of gifts that might lure the spirit from the patient. The tray held a little brown paper packet containing aniseed, an envelope full of saffron, flakes of pungent resin and a few tempting little morsels – a banana, some grains of maize, a fresh egg.

The *mtege* or patient whom the healer produced for us was a young woman. Led gently forward, her head covered in a suli, a red Swahili scarf, she was quivering, her mind allegedly lost. Then the music struck up, ringing and pounding from a brass cymbal and two goatskin and sisal drums. It was frenetic, changing rhythms continuously, searching for a response in the girl. I was soon lost in the compelling beat and it was only minutes before the girl too was swaying – only held upright, it seemed, by the thickness of the hypnotic music in the morning air. The sound of drumming was immeasurably old – what to me as a boy would have seemed like the sound of Africa itself.

Suddenly the girl collapsed, releasing two shuddering yells from deep inside. The *mganga* grabbed a bottle – I noticed it was labelled 'Smirnoff Vodka' – and pressed it to her forehead before deftly spinning it on its little metal lid. The spirit was safely captured inside. For this spirit originates from the Arab side of the Swahili heritage, and is the evil 'jinn' about which the Koran gives guidance – that untrustworthy giant Jinni which emerged from young Aladdin's magic lamp.

I left the village – with the girl back to normal rather too miraculously and the Smirnoff bottle lying in the dust, lid still tightly screwed on – and began thinking about my forthcoming railway journey, and the Victorian explorers who had opened up the country. They would have called these rituals mumbo-jumbo, native superstition. Yet as a so-called modern-day explorer I've spent the past twelve years sinking into tribal societies, and I now see them as our key to understanding the world's remote areas. These rituals may look strange, if not downright bizarre, but I've seen very real cures enacted on people who have long since given up on Western medicine.

As city gives way to countryside, a colourful group of young
Kenyans turn out to greet the travellers

I might have dreamt of going to the Mountains of the Moon since
boyhood, but arriving at the station to start my journey I was apprehensive. My
sort of travel is paddling a dugout canoe quietly up a creek – or more likely just
sinking into some timeless tribal world, and sitting getting cramp during their
rather long rituals. But trains mean timetables, and I don't even wear a watch.
Trains mean travelling companions, and I always travel alone. Trains mean a
fixed route, and I like to travel wherever the terrain seems to guide me. But
I'd been shot at in the Amazon and poisoned in Peru, and I supposed I'd get
through this somehow.

Once upon a time the railway had been the leading edge of change in
East Africa. Now, a hundred years since construction started, Mombasa is a
package tour destination and I had to barge through clumps of tourists on the
platform. It was the railway that had been left clinging lamely to values, and
rolling stock, from a bygone British era. As the diesel pulled us out of the
station and we clacked over the points, still gathering speed, I got out my

notebook and did a tally of the foreigners who were on board with me, most of them wedged up and down the narrow corridors and craning from windows: backpackers, six; middle-aged safari tourists in shorts, fourteen; lager louts, twelve; suburban housewives enjoying illicit flings with Mombasa beach boys, two; finally film crews, one.

The train was swiftly out of Mombasa and now heading resolutely into the countryside, stirring dust over the maize crops, rattling the back yards of the African poor. Children ran alongside, hands out, begging for loose change. The safari tourists flung them sandwiches from their packed lunches, the backpackers tossed biscuits, the lager louts just cheerily waved back. And me? I was lost in my own thoughts – this journey was as alive with the spirits of the dead as it was with the spirits of the living. It wasn't a ghost train, but for me the line was haunted – it mirrored too closely the journeys of too many of my explorer predecessors.

Originally the British government had been reluctant to get involved out here in East Africa, which didn't seem to offer much more than the dreaded Masai tribesmen and a range of unidentified fevers. But the travels of the missionary-explorer David Livingstone and others drew attention to the Arab slave trade. He gradually swayed moral opinion, in 1857 calling on 'commerce and Christianity' to open up the interior. Perhaps more to the point as far as the British were concerned, the Scramble for Africa was soon under way among would-be colonial powers. In 1886 an Anglo-German Agreement divided up East Africa into two spheres of influence. The Imperial British East Africa Company set about building a railway into the interior, a £5 million project which had to negotiate the Taru Desert, just inland, then the huge Rift Valley, marauding animals and – horror of horrors at the time – those Masai. The railway builders had hardly left Mombasa before over half their workforce had gone down with dysentery, malaria and sleeping sickness. Over two years, most of their livestock was also lost to disease and pests. It wasn't long before the railway was dubbed 'the Lunatic Line'.

I settled myself into my empty upper-class carriage, unpacking the hefty books which I'd brought along, rather ambitiously, in the hope of reading them on the journey. They consisted of the works of miscellaneous Victorian pioneers and I began pondering about the weight of all this British legacy on

Africa – only to discover that this particular train wasn't a vestige of our empire at all. It was built in 1978 in Pennsylvania, USA.

Having just opened the first worthy tome, Verney Lovett Cameron's *Across Africa*, I found it was time to get off the train. This was Voi, and all around us lay Tsavo National Park, the largest game park in Kenya: over 8000 square miles of dry savannah with four hundred species of bird and sixty species of mammal, including eight thousand elephants. But to the railway construction crew it was just an obstacle, one early hurdle of many hundreds. On reaching Tsavo they were plagued by two man-eating lionesses. At night the labourers took to building thorn-bush defences around their camps, like the Masai. It didn't do much good. One by one the imported Indian labourers were dragged away or chewed on the spot. Twenty-eight men were killed before the beasts were hunted down. Then a Superintendent Ryall was brought in to shoot a third lion, a 'terrible brute'. But the 'Kima Killer' nabbed him as well, dragging the good policeman out of his railway carriage window.

The current Head Warden of Tsavo, Mr Gichange, whisked me off in his Land Cruiser to see his elephants, right in the middle of the plain. When we got there I discovered it wasn't quite as romantic an idea as it had seemed. I was wearing my only good shirt, and the elephants were orphans apparently in need of physical comfort. They were just finishing their mudbath. While the elephants sprayed me with brick-red silt and meticulously sucked the polish off my shoes, the warden started to give me all the usual stuff about Tsavo being a success story: no more poaching . . . elephant population booming . . . rhinos reintroduced . . . compensation if villagers' crops trampled. I'd heard all this before, and it's too neat an answer to a complex ecological problem.

Kenya still has one of the highest population growths in the world. The situation in the local community of Voi is typical. More and more land is required, and the fences being erected to prevent wildlife destroying local crops are not going to contain the problem for ever. It's a human timebomb, and it was set ticking by an overcrowded Europe which wants a spacious theme park, a raw, natural arena. Meanwhile Kenya plays a dangerous game, peddling our urban desires, making a living out of our dreams, while we show every sign of wanting nature more than the people whose home Africa is.

Back at Voi Station the train onward to Nairobi was due at eleven that evening, and was already late. I did what everyone else seemed to be doing and settled down on the platform for the night. The women, some of them with heaps of market produce, others with empty bags to fill, laid themselves out gently to sleep under the iridescent moon. A silence descended on us. There were only the insects and the trackside frogs, and their sounds in the darkness were smoothing, a blanket over us. I was glad for a chance to be still, to be absorbed by Africa before rattling onward again. After a while sitting in this peace, I didn't want the train to come at all.

On board the night train when it eventually arrived, the man who came to make my bed was a Masai – a *moran*, or man from their warrior class. Once these men, the knife edge of a fiercely proud, pastoral society, had been the great fear of the Indian railway workers, but now they worked on the railway themselves. For decades the presence of the Masai in the vast tracts of land between Lake Victoria and the coast had blocked all exploration of what is today Kenya, and it was only when the Masai were weakened by both internal feuding and a series of crippling epidemics that the British were able to negotiate a treaty that allowed the railway to come through. For the Masai that treaty proved costly indeed. Not only did the railway carve through their heartlands, but it encouraged white settlers, who were soon shifting them off their grazing lands.

I drifted off to sleep thinking about how I'd been mothered by a Masai 'warrior' – he'd even told me how to get into bed. It's an effect I always seem to have on tribal people. They take me in because I don't appear threatening – I'm not the missionary with *Good News*, not the scientist with strange gadgets. On the other hand, I thought, as the train swayed around another corner, rolling me over in my bunk, perhaps these tribal people just think I'm helpless and don't want me to die on their hands.

By morning I felt refreshed and almost ready for the horrors of Nairobi. I wasn't looking forward to the capital – one more Third World honeypot city, remorselessly drawing in the rural young. In 1899, when the railway reached here, Nairobi was nothing more than a Masai marsh, a spot for watering cattle. Now it was a city of 2 million. For the railway had left behind more than some interesting old rolling stock and a slowish service to a lake in Uganda. Its

ABOVE Meeting Richard Leakey: palaeontologist, conservationist
and politician in a dangerous country

OPPOSITE Noisy, throbbing River Road – although this is central
Nairobi, street crime and poverty abound

creation brought in European farmers who were quick to exploit the fertile uplands, and Indians who largely run the country's business community. In fact it brought modern Kenya. 'It is not an uncommon thing for a line to open up a country,' wrote Sir Charles Eliot, Commissioner of the British East Africa Protectorate from 1901 to 1904, 'but this line literally created a country.'

In River Road, more than anywhere else, you can feel the drumbeat of modern Africa – the exciting energy throbbing from the hawkers and drivers of *matatus*, the shared car or minicab that is a common mode of transport in this region. It's the city centre, not an outer slum. Yet a fleet of boys waits to beg; a child with only a banana to sell pleads with each of us in turn. Before venturing here we took off our wristwatches and other valuables, and hired minders to stand by the cameraman. The city is buckling under the strain of a population that doubles in size every twelve years. Too many people search for too few jobs. Protestant churches spring up everywhere as the old certainties of tribal values give way to confusion and disillusionment. The crime rate is soaring, and corruption in government rife.

But let's try to be positive. A melting pot? Not a bit. Still, even thirty-two years after independence, if you ask anyone their origin they say Kikuyu, or Luo, or one of over seventy other tribes – not 'Kenyan'. It was like that here in River Road, and it was like that at the Hilton – people had lost interest in any leadership offered from the top and were getting on with trying to make a living for themselves and their own kind. Sorry, but it has to be said. More bad news for Africa.

To address these problems one of Kenya's best-known white citizens, Richard Leakey, is now spearheading a new political party. Safina, as the organization is called, hopes to attract followers from both black and white communities, and to make a stand against the rampant state corruption. It is a dangerous plan in a country where political opponents have been known to die suddenly of unnatural causes. But Leakey is not a man to duck issues. Until recently he was head of the Kenya Wildlife Service and in this capacity was responsible for eliminating the wholesale poaching of elephants. All this aside, his excavations of early human remains also put him, to my mind, in the forefront of modern exploration, so I was determined to meet him. River Road wasn't a good idea as a rendezvous. Somehow we ended up meeting in just the sort of place both of us had spent our lives getting away from: a neatly trimmed, blooming garden near the writer Karen Blixen's former farmhouse, in what is now a safe white suburban enclave.

He was taller than I'd expected, and rather cunning and smooth in front of the camera. I soon saw that I wasn't going to crack the veneer of this tough old politico. Rather unexpectedly, though, I did make one scratch. I'd asked why man evolved in Africa – not, for instance Asia, or the Thames Valley for that matter. He answered a little casually, opening himself up like one of those tribesmen who felt I wasn't a threat. He just said, 'Benedict, it's sometimes more important to ask "how" questions than "why" questions.' It was an evasive and lazy response, and one which allowed me to say that surely asking questions was what drove him as a palaeontologist at Lake Turkana – in fact, what enabled man to spread out from Africa in the first place. But I admired Leakey and his dogged strength – if he got into power, no one was going to corrupt *him*. And he'd been tolerant of me, still green out here. I ended with a nice'n'easy interview-round-up question. Did he, as a former palaeontologist, perhaps have a dream left? Finding a special bit of humanoid skull, perhaps . . .?

'If we can show man has a common origin,' he said, raising a telling finger in the air, '*then* we can convince people that we have a common destiny . . .' The more I thought about that one, the less happy I was. To talk of a common destiny is wonderful rhetoric, but what does it mean to the average hungry African? And will the white man then still be setting the agenda, as he did with his expeditions and railways – even with his race meetings? For today was Derby Day, and everyone was heading to the racecourse for a flutter. I was keen to see how another element of Kenya, 'Keenyans' (to use the old colonial pronunciation), were faring. Like the black tribes, the values of the closed white communities were under threat as the nation struggled to redefine itself.

The racecourse was much as I had expected – the manicured lawns, the Derby Day dresses. But I found it no longer a white man's world. This was the new Kenya, a burgeoning black middle class. Here I noticed a new confidence

OVERLEAF **A day at the races: formerly the exclusive preserve of rich whites, the Nairobi racecourse is now a playground for middle-class black Africans**

among young Kenyans – people self-made, not given a hand-up by the white community, people who'd now got something of their own behind them. At the racecourse, whatever your origin, you were now able to suffer together from the tone-deaf strains of the third-rate African singer who served as lunchtime entertainment. Alternatively, you were free to struggle as I did to work out the Indian bookies' betting system. In the end I put all of $2 on the Big Race. I lost, of course, but came away feeling a little better about Kenya. Even in this most exclusive of circles, now all that separated you from the elite was money.

The next morning I was back at Nairobi Station, where I had arranged a detour up north to Isiolo to visit some Masai friends. A few months ago they had bought some camels and as I was preparing for my next expedition, a trek with my own camels up southern Africa's Namib Desert, I'd joined them to get some training in. Now I wanted to get a lift back up there on a goods train, and say a brief farewell. It was early, a moment of tranquillity before the departure of passenger trains. A lone sweeper was shifting the dust off the platform on to the tracks. And down on the tracks, a man in gumboots was whimsically flagging various stray pieces of rolling stock into place.

The long train wound its way north, its empty carriages swaying, me hanging on tight in one of them. Ahead was Mount Kenya, a ragged blue ridge; around me rich ochre soils and green shoots thickening now with the first rains. This was more like it, as far as I was concerned – a spacious goods wagon with wide open doors, freedom just to swing my legs in the breeze, to wave to passing strangers as they looked up from their fields. And that most exhilarating pleasure for the traveller: watching stony, suspicious faces break slowly into answering smiles, that spark of humanity jumping between two different worlds.

When German missionaries first recorded the snowy peaks of Kilimanjaro and Mount Kenya in the 1840s they were ridiculed. Snow? On the Equator! But some geographers began to wonder. Perhaps these were the Mountains of the Moon, the fabled source of the Nile. In 1856 Richard Burton and John Hanning Speke set off to find the source and settle its whereabouts, once and for all. Before long, they were also bickering. The only two white men in the East African interior, and they wouldn't talk to each other.

One thing they did agree about – you didn't get to the source of the Nile by coming directly west from the coast through here. As the explorer Henry Morton Stanley pointed out, only those looking for quick martyrdom should come direct through Masailand. Most explorers carefully entered the interior from Zanzibar, to the south. But in 1878 Joseph Thomson, though only twenty-six, took up the challenge. He was stalked much of the way by the Masai – and survived by behaving with considerably less arrogance than average for the era: he entertained them by removing his false teeth. I didn't have any of those, unfortunately. And I sat in my goods wagon wondering if I could improve on my own party trick, at the moment a rather pitiful rendition of 'Old MacDonald Had a Farm'.

At the station I was reunited with the film crew. We bucked along in two Land Rovers, dodging the savannah anthills until at last I saw through the scrub the red of the Masai wraps and the flash of their spear blades. From childhood, your life as a Masai is divided into clearly defined stages. My friends were all *moran*, young men who spend all day guarding cattle, their family's wealth. They're 'twenty-somethings', living the time of their lives away from the duties of the village. Women aren't allowed here, but the *moran* confided that actually they all have secret girlfriends.

I couldn't help but be uneasy, bringing the film crew along. But I wanted to get Masai on camera, to show them as people, not as tourist attractions, as noble, rather sexy, warriors – picture postcard takeaways. As it happened, they were just as keen on checking out the film crew as the film crew were to check out them. At first, both regarded each other with exactly the same degree of suspicion and fascination. But a young *moran* called Dawani was soon using the cameraman's lens as a mirror to adjust the sprig of Christmas gold tinsel he wore in his hair. The rest stood chatting about us with their legs casually crossed, like Roman legionaries – except that they were gently holding hands or preening their long braided hair, of which they were immensely proud. Soon I was catching up on gossip with my closest friend among them, David Lege. He had had a bit of bad news: his father had decided it was time for him to marry. So he'd had to follow tradition and cut off his precious hair. His days as a *moran*, sleeping on a goatskin under the sun and stars, had finally come to an end.

The camels which had originally brought us together were unusual for the Masai, who hoped to use them to help lug water up from the river. The creatures had been in training for several weeks since I'd last seen them, but still they didn't seem to have learnt a thing. Knowing something about camels myself, I tried to help break in the young ones. I didn't have a saddle or full bridle, and the first pupil just stood stock still like a stubborn mule. The second skilfully humped his hairy hump higher and made me slide off; the third folded up under my weight. Through all of this, they gurgled away as contentedly as ever. I found it reassuring that the Masai were having as much difficulty as I.

At dusk the cattle were steered from the savannah into the safety of the thorn bush *boma* or kraal. The men sang unselfconsciously for each other as they stoked the fire. Later they chanted, the sound steadily gathering force like a wind, their guttural voices working around us, seeming to fend off whatever might be out there in the night and to pull us closer to the sparking fire and the African soil. The more I began to settle in with the *moran*, the more content I was. This was travel for me: not movement but stillness. Not passing by, but passing into. These Masai are a window into this landscape. Their cow-dung houses and goatskin beds look primitive but are merely the marks of a society that specializes in mobility. Their investment isn't in bricks and mortar but in cattle – their daily source of food, their larders through times of drought – and in the savannah that sustains these herds. This relationship gives the Masai an intimacy with the landscape that we can never hope to gain. But even they are beginning to succumb to our relentless invasion. Ever since the railway thrust into East Africa, they've had sufficient pride to resist Western dress and all the tempting goodies we've brought. But now even they have their sights set on watches and TVs. That's understandable – but there's so much for us to learn before they pack their bags.

All too soon I was back in Nairobi and on course again for Uganda. Leaving the capital, the train gave us a panoramic view. This was unfortunate, because what we saw was Kibera Estate – a suburb which is, when all's said and done, a shanty town. Huts were walled with polythene bags, roofs beaten from diesel drums. The mud on the tracks from all the shoeless urchins made our train slip. I wondered if, or when, those Masai would end up living like these people – at the bottom of a man-made heap, ensnared by Western dreams.

Over lunch on the train to Uganda, Millie Muyoti expounded her views
on women's natural suitability for management roles

Inside the upper-class carriage, the colonial cocoon, you could easily
forget about the cloud hanging over the country: fourteen of the world's
sixteen poorest countries are in this continent and Kenya, though still wealthy,
is no longer one of post-independent Africa's shining lights. It too is teetering;
the fear is that it may even join that list. It was lunchtime, and as far as the
white-suited waiters were concerned there was nothing unusual in the view –
and anyway there was starched white linen to spread, curled napkins to place.
I carefully selected my dining companion: an extremely modern and intriguing
female called Miss Millie Muyoti, who ran the Nairobi Hilton poolside bar. By
the time we got to 'dessert' Millie and I were getting on rather well, I thought.
Soon she was showing me her way of cutting a mango, and we were talking
about how women the world over are taught to be managers. In third class,
down the corridor, even the female toddlers were busy managing the babies.
And by the time the girls were thirteen or fourteen – old enough when
travelling to balance the inevitable Kenyan mattress on their head – they led

a whole cohort of children. 'Ah, yes,' we sighed – I'm afraid by now half cut on the cheap red wine – 'once the world's in the hands of women, then we'll get along much better all round.'

Out of the window, I saw I was missing the Rift Valley. I dashed to put my head out and savour this huge geological fault-line running up Africa from Mozambique to Israel's Dead Sea. Here the giant trough was a smooth spread of farmland of billiard-table green reaching to magnificent Longonot, the coned mountain which posed artfully behind. Further south were the barren earth sites of Olduvai Gorge, where Richard Leakey's father, Louis, had scratched away to uncover man's origins. My own father was an airline pilot out in East Africa, and when I was eleven and he brought me for a glimpse of the continent he chose a view of the Serengeti Plains, which touch the Rift Valley to the south.

Finally the train began to ascend the precipitous Mau Escarpment, lacing up through conifers pointing from burnt sienna soil, tall grasses with the afternoon's rain still dripping off the blades. We climbed and we climbed. Children ran alongside, cheering the train on. I thought again of the poor old railway construction crew – the periodic floods which washed away the lines and the plagues of caterpillars squelching under the wheels and making them spin.

By night we were crossing the border into Uganda. The only bit of the train without electricity was upper class. I couldn't see a thing in the dark, but it didn't bother the Kenyan frontier official. He contentedly entered my pitch-black cabin and stamped my passport without seeming to notice. The Ugandan official wasn't so easy. Perhaps he was scared of the dark. He sent a minion down the corridor to drag me out – and I'm never at my best at three in the morning.

As the train trundled onwards, elephant grass clattered on the windows. I managed a couple more hours' sleep – though by now I was eager for morning and my first sight of Uganda. In the morning I opened my window to find the soil darker. Steam percolated through homely grass hut roofs and sleepy brown cows stood about, looking clean from the rain. This was the country which Winston Churchill called the Pearl of Africa. And oddly enough, this side of the border did seem to have grown more lush, more fertile. Maize flourished, children sang out. The Ugandans had suffered for years under bloody dictators but the land had never failed them. In much of the rest of Africa, tens of thousands had died of starvation.

We were heading for Jinja, the closest station to the Nile's source. After many wanderings in search of this spot, in 1958 Burton and Speke discovered Lake Tanganyika, which Burton believed to be the source. By now they were weak and sick – Burton's legs were paralysed, Speke half blind from ophthalmia and deaf from an insect burrowing into his ear. They headed back, east towards the coast, stopping at the Arab trading post of Tabora. Here, Speke decided to head off alone to investigate their stories of a second lake to the north, which was the real source. Eventually, his eyes still weak, he arrived at the lake that he was to name Victoria. This was his great moment – and he was steered there on the back of a donkey, wearing sunglasses. The locals called him 'double eyes'.

Coming out of Jinja Station I found that the local form of transport had been updated – to a bicycle. After all that the nineteenth-century explorers had been through to reach this point, it seemed unfitting to hop on to a bicycle made for two. But before long I was at last padding about on the rocky bank of Lake Victoria. I'd been expecting the source to be a glistening cascade of water flowing out of the lake. Instead, the Ripon Falls consisted of a murky river containing a few rocks, on one of which a man in an ailing tree was stealing birds' eggs. Frankly it was a bit of a let-down. And not far down river another disappointment was awaiting me – the Owen Falls Hydroelectric Dam. Now the great river was subject to the whims of the capital's electricity consumers – the Nile available at the turn of a tap.

It was years before Speke's findings were accepted. He returned to Africa in 1860 with James Grant and found this spot, but even then went back to England without sufficient proof to establish that it was indeed the source of the Nile. David Livingstone, the most prestigious explorer of the time, was called in to settle the matter. But the great man died in 1873 near Lake Bangweulu, investigating a tributary of the Upper Congo – 600 miles off target.

OVERLEAF **Crossing the White Nile at Jinja. Victorian explorers endured tropical diseases and great hardship in their attempts to find the source of the Nile**

Winding around the shimmering waters and towering reed beds of Lake Victoria, the train took us on towards the capital, Kampala. Passengers hung from the doors and poked out of windows, enjoying the breeze and chewing sugar cane. I was more than happy to be on my way again, back on that line to the Mountains of the Moon. There was something about these mountains that encapsulated all that the Europeans were searching for – and perhaps still are. Whether on package tours or wildlife safaris, we look to Africa to provide a spectacle that's awesome and romantic, perhaps even fearsome. The continent serves us as a resource. We need to believe there's somewhere worse off than us – a place of cannibals, of darkness, that can benefit from our values. And, paradoxically, we also need somewhere to dream about, an Eden, a Paradise – that word comes from Old Persian in which it meant, literally, 'park'. And way back in time, Europeans began to feel that Africa fitted the bill nicely. It gradually became the Dark Continent.

As for us explorers, the agents charged by Western society to dispel these dreams, it's odd how little actual exploring we've done. When we first arrived here Africa was already well known, not just by the Africans whose home it was but also by the Arabs, who already had well-established slaving routes and acted as guides to the West's most famous explorers. And are we any better now, in our computer-driven, 'enlightened' scientific age? We still bring along our compasses and charts, extending our Western, rationalizing view of the world just as Victorian England forged this railway line, a piece of late Victorian England, into the interior of another world.

Up in the trees children, crouched in their rags like birds of prey, were munching freshly picked fruit. Women lifted their babies, showing them the train. An old dear sat knocking two sticks together, sitting contentedly in a heap amid someone's vegetable patch. Ordinary scenes of humanity, yet to me 'Uganda' meant, more than anything, disaster and mayhem. The first Prime Minister of independent Uganda, Milton Obote, abolished the monarchy and created a one-party state. His overthrow by Idi Amin had come as a relief. Then there was 'Field Marshal' Amin himself, the man who kept human heads in his fridge, who got someone to drive a car over his archbishop. After a 'liberating' invasion from Tanzania and the ousting of Amin in 1979 there were a couple of very temporary heads of states – and then back to Obote again . . .

As we slowed down on the approach to Kampala, we wound past the rubbish dump homes of marabou storks; I braced myself for the worst. However, it soon became obvious that the city was a good deal more civil than Nairobi. The President for the last ten years, the former resistance leader Yoweri Museveni, had led the country out of the abyss. One of Amin's inspirations, some sort of towering Islamic minaret, still stood there half-built in its scaffolding and was now mocking its creator – as were the markets, flourishing once again. Now you could buy everything you wanted, from garlic to grasshoppers. The insects were certainly juicy-looking, if rather a bright green. They were available per kilo, legs still on; or, if you preferred, legs yanked off and ready to eat.

But could the past be so easily forgotten? What about the sixty thousand Asians whom in 1972 Amin was told in a dream to throw out? I found the old Indian quarter, but its Art Deco houses were mottled ochre with dust and mostly boarded up. The only faces around were African. I went along to the Hindu temple, surely the hub of any surviving community.

The priest introduced me to a Mr Ruparalia, and while the first candles were being lit for evening prayer we found a quiet place behind a statue of a resplendent sacred cow and sat down on the floor. He talked of Amin – awarded by the people the title of *kijambiya*, or slaughterer; of how Mr Ruparalia himself had avoided eviction because he had a Ugandan passport; of seeing his relations off to the airport, day by day; of the day his cousin's body turned up in the papyrus reed beds of Lake Victoria. Ironically, the streets in those days were free of crime – no one, but no one, dared risk a trip to the police jails. Mr Ruparalia had clung on. Hitler had been ousted, his reasoning went, so surely the fool Amin would go soon. This was, after all, the man who had to inspect his tanks on a bicycle because there was no longer any petrol.

When the bell for prayers rang out, only half a dozen young men trickled into the huge building for worship. But the community was growing now, and there was no doubt in anyone's mind that the temple would one day be full again.

My next port of call was the Kabaka tombs, the burial place of the kings of Buganda. The regional kingdoms had emerged in the fourteenth and fifteenth centuries from a melting pot of Nilotic-speaking cattle herders and

ABOVE Passengers on a train in Uganda

OPPOSITE Kampala Station, bright with the robes and possessions
of crowds of travelling Africans

54

Bantu-speaking agriculturalists, and before the monarchy was abolished in 1967 the Bugandans had been the most powerful of the four. The building was essentially a huge mound of simply laid thatch, but there was also a sense of majesty here. Every element of the structure threw up these contrasts – it was neither formal nor informal, neither palace nor hut. One of the most interesting things about the accounts of the explorers Speke and Grant, the first Europeans to arrive here, was their surprise at finding a sophisticated royal court with much of the complicated state ritual to be seen in any European equivalent. This was civilization – though it turned out that King Mtesa did roast his subjects alive. And when Speke presented him with a pistol he ordered a pageboy to go away and test it by shooting someone.

The tombs themselves remain unseen behind barkcloth screens. Only the kings' portraits are visible, along with mementoes left by passing explorers: a cannon said to have been dropped off by Stanley, also oil lamps and chairs – a mere token of the empire which was to be brought along in due course. Four women sat on the floor, diligently weaving mats. They were descendants of the Bugandan kings' wives, guardians of the tombs. They wove continually for no apparent reason. I coaxed them to tell me why, but came away with no satisfactory answer. Perhaps I'd have got further if I'd asked a 'how' question instead of a 'why' question.

Back to Kampala Station for the last leg of my rail journey. Although the original line finished at Lake Victoria the train now runs on to Kasese and the Ruwenzoris, those Mountains of the Moon. An easy enough trip, I thought, but the head of Uganda Railways himself advised our film producer against it. Still, it couldn't be that bad, could it?

I was the only white man on the densely packed platform – the film crew had decided to stay well clear, across the tracks. I was easy prey for hawkers, who began trying to sell me jeans apparently designed for dwarves. The journey started ominously, with the train arriving backwards – and not exactly roaring into action. The crowds surged. As I squeezed on board, my wallet was removed with admirable professionalism. I now had diarrhoea, and heaven knows how long the queue would be for the toilets. I was beginning to see why the BBC always booked me into first class – and here there was no option but third.

I was wrong about having to queue for the loos – there weren't any. The train was so full that they acted as extra accommodation. This was an East German train, and in East Germany, it seems, they don't design trains to cope with excess Ugandans returning home for a weekend break.

It was a long haul to Kasese, and there were several stops for sustenance when everyone scrambled off the train to buy a stick of sugarcane. But they'd hardly set foot on the tracks than it was time for them to squeeze on board again. I stood around with the rest of the passengers, who all seemed to be hawkers selling those dwarf jeans. One by one we made a bid for the breeze that was slipping in through the diesel-stained, sometimes bullet-holed, windows. 'We get there, slowly by slowly,' one fellow sufferer said to me. But he didn't sound convinced. I did at least rub shoulders with many ordinary Ugandans, and began again to feel their optimism for the future. The liberal Museveni was thought a 'miracle'. The newly restored monarchy was also something they were proud of – and seemed to gain strength from.

As we crept nearer and nearer the great mountain range, the countryside grew greener. So did the tracks. I began to think a train had never passed this way before. Seeing us, field labourers dropped their hoes and stood in rapt attention. Children stopped their football and leaned against the goalposts, which were invariably sprouting shoots. Some time during the night the train crunched to a halt and wouldn't budge. A previous train had been stranded since heaven knows how long ago up the line. Our engine went wandering off into the night to see if the way was clear, and we were left alone in the darkness. At dawn we were still there. We sat around in the damp with the swamp frogs, wondering what next. I'd only been travelling a few weeks, and already I felt I needed a holiday.

We set off again quite some time later, and now I was straining for the first sight of the mountains. This stretch of the line was built forty years ago to bring copper from the Kasese mines. But it was bringing me to see the range talked about for almost two thousand years.

OVERLEAF **A group of elephants take their morning walk to a watering-hole. White Europeans have a very different view of wildlife from the Africans who have to share their land with it**

At last we pulled into Kasese – the end of the line, the train, and the European advance, forced to a halt by the mountains. When Victorian explorers like Speke, Grant and Stanley reached the region we now call Uganda, they were granted an audience with the King of Buganda. And I had managed to fix up an audience with a princess of Toro, one of the other kingdoms. She was Princess Elizabeth, a former Ambassador to Washington and even Foreign Minister under Amin – until he chucked her out and took that post for himself as well.

We'd arranged to meet in her palace. It all sounded very promising. The film crew lent me a shirt, and I accosted a hotel waitress who agreed to hire out her husband's tie at $1.50 a day. As we set off, we were slightly in trepidation. But the palace wasn't quite what we were expecting. Perched up on the hill it had been, like the age-old monarchy, seen as a symbol of unity in the country, and had therefore been targeted for destruction. Obote had started to demolish the palace in 1967, when he dissolved the monarchy; it suffered further when Amin's troops took it over, and further still at the time of the Tanzanian invasion to get rid of the dictator.

The palace was therefore a sad ruin – but the Princess was far from a disappointment. An impressive figure, all the more so for sitting in a heap of rubble, she spoke of her hopes for the country and of the exciting energy that I too had felt here. Uganda was something good to talk about in what was otherwise a mess of a continent. The nation was pulling together, facing up to its problems. Here there were street signs telling you 'My friend with AIDS is still a friend', reminding you that 2 million of the 19 million population were infected. I admired the Ugandans, and was pleased with the puzzle they'd set me: were they such a resilient people because they had been strengthened by adversity? Or was this some ancient characteristic of their race – the strength of mind of King Mtesa, who held the European explorers for five months before allowing poor old Speke a dash to that Nile source at long last?

The Ugandans were picking up the pieces, re-establishing their links with the past – as I had done on this journey. I found this a reassuring thought as I went off to complete my pilgrimage to the mountains. I walked up towards the clouds hanging from the ridges. Swallows were swinging from holes in the rock – old copper and cobalt workings; a little girl was ferrying maize to her chickens in a now disused army hat. The 60-mile-long range stretched out around me, the steep lower flanks mist-wrapped, the summits themselves totally lost in the heavens. However far I walked towards them, the crags always seemed to be the same distance away – out of reach. Many of the central peaks carried the names of the Europeans who once sought them out – Mount Speke, Mount Stanley, Mount Baker – but even though they now bore Western nametags they seemed to be as elusive as they always had been.

Up and up the road I went through the village of Kilembe mines. A girl skipped by in a Sunday dress, slowed by the weight of a huge black Bible. Up on the hill slopes, a man stood up to his knees in mud; he was taking a rest, watching as his wife dug the wet soil. A vehicle rumbled by with no exhaust pipe. On one of its buckled doors a sentence in enamel paint read: 'My car is protected by the blood of Jesus Christ.' Slowly, all these things disappeared out of sight as I climbed up the road.

This was only a short walk into the foothills, but it was something a hundred generations of Europeans had only ever been able to dream about. More than anything, coming up into the blue, reptilian range, the mists unveiling and veiling the crags, you sense a feeling of awe and mystery. And ironically, that's exactly what Western exploration has always been dedicated to getting rid of. It was something always understood by the Africans: if we question the forces that govern our lives, we start to erode our respect for them. I was glad to have found the place before me still a little unexplored. On reaching these mountains, man has been stopped in his tracks. His machines are useless, and the range is too big to bulldoze. He is forced to stop imposing with his railways and ideas, and to listen. It is as it should be: man standing back like a child before the beating heart of the great continent itself.

Crewe to Crewe via Scotland

VICTORIA WOOD

I START MY JOURNEY at Crewe Station, traditionally the centre of the British rail network. 'Ooh, yes, I know Crewe terribly well', but once I arrive and look about me I realize I have never set foot in it. I see now what I have missed by turning down Paraguay and Vietnam and all those other exotic rail journeys. There is no drama here: no one is gesturing histrionically, or talking animatedly, or embracing. We are all British and we have faces like scones, plates or baked potatoes. If a train is late we will tut and sigh, working in pairs if possible. If an announcement is made to the effect that Cheshire and the North Midlands have been seized by a military dictator basing himself in Nantwich, we will look at our watches and say, 'There goes my Yogaerobics.'

The station is freezing. That's the trouble with stations – there have to be holes to let the trains in and out. There seem to be a lot of personnel around, all in jaunty blazers like Butlin's Redcoats. I worry at first that under John Major's Citizens' Charter they are there to make us enjoy ourselves, while we're waiting; but they only seem to be giving directions, rather than badgering anyone to do Olde Tyme Dancing or decorate wooden spoons. I do a piece to camera next to two very nicely made-up ladies on a bench. They have overnight bags, but I restrain myself from questioning them as to their sexual

Victoria Wood about to leave Crewe in Cheshire, known for a century and more as the hub of Britain's railway system

habits and plans for the evening. They don't seem to mind being filmed, so presumably they are not a pair of small-boned transvestites taking a day off from the office.

There's a nun in the buffet in a contemporary beige outfit – blouse, skirt and one of those head-dresses you see in catering uniform catalogues. I wonder, is there a nun section in one of those catalogues? Or does the Church merit its own publication – lady vicars in jaunty pastel dog collars, captured by the cameras in typical pose, blessing a parishioner, stocktaking the communion wafers? I don't like to ask.

In the buffet I'm nabbed by a Scotsman who has been availing himself of the alcoholic and non-alcoholic drinks served by 'our friendly and helpful staff'. He gets on the train with me and keeps holding my hand, telling me I am magic, and offers me five pounds for charity. I hold his lager while he fumbles with a roll of tenners. I have to borrow a fiver from the director to give him his change . . . and I've just realized that the money the Scotsman gave me has ended up in the washing machine.

We wave him goodbye at Lancaster. Lancaster is a well-kept, solid, respectable sort of station – I used to commute to London from here and, waiting now for the Carnforth train to go north, I feel I'm on the wrong platform. Carnforth is the station where they filmed the exteriors for the classic David Lean film of 1945 *Brief Encounter*. The station is a mess – no ticket office, toilets or buffet. The platforms have wire fencing along them, presumably to stop you emulating the distraught Celia. (Though in fact she does pull back from chucking herself under the express and returns to her husband. Quite right too.)

The only reminder of the film is the huge clock suspended over the ramp which leads to the far platforms. The clock still goes, but the time is wrong. I talk to Elaine Maudsley, who worked at Carnforth buffet during the war for ten shillings a week, and was an extra in *Brief Encounter* for thirty-five shillings a night. The cab the BBC has booked to bring her to the station has refused to come, as the driver is not convinced the BBC will stump up the £1.80 fare. This story comes as no surprise to anyone who's ever lived there.

Fifty years ago Elaine Maudsley worked as an extra on *Brief Encounter*, which was filmed here at Carnforth: the station clock is the only relic of those days

We stroll up and down the platform as she tells me about how thrilled she was to be an extra, and how she wore the same clothes to be married in. She's lived in Carnforth all her life and is incensed by the way the station has been allowed to deteriorate. I don't understand it myself. On the way up we passed a signal box which had been reopened as a Heritage Centre. You'd think Carnforth would be a gift for the nostalgia boom. It's got the lot – steam trains, the war, Noël Coward, Rachmaninov. You could have a buffet where the spoon was on a chain and people behind the counter going 'Don't you know there's a war on?' every time you asked for anything.

Carnforth today is looking unusually prosperous, with all the shops in business. Over the years, when I lived here, I got used to new businesses failing soon after opening. In fact, shops would often open with a sticker over the window: 'CLOSING SHORTLY'. At lunchtime I have a soup at Loveday's Café and see three old friends. The crew are very impressed by my local popularity and I don't tell them that these are the only three people I know between here and Dundee.

It's mid-afternoon and very sunny, and the tide is out on Morecambe Bay. It's a spectacularly beautiful place, with a quality to the light I've never seen captured in a painting. I feel very odd as we pass through Silverdale where I used to live, and still miss badly. I would hear the trains as I lay in bed at night.

The station at Grange-over-Sands is very picturesque, with lovely stone windows looking out over the bay. The day I moved away from Silverdale four years ago I walked across the bay to Grange with Cedric Robinson, the Queen's Sand Pilot (he leads people across the bay: he knows all the safe places to cross). The Queen wasn't of the party, but I think Prince Philip has crossed the sands in some equipage involving whips and bowler hats. The train hugs the coastline all the way to Barrow-in-Furness, and then travels on to Carlisle, where the driver tells me he knows a man who bought my washing machine. I forget to ask him if it's still working.

At Carlisle we have appealed for train spotters on local radio. I am approached by an elderly woman who is train spotting on behalf of her deceased husband. She'd heard something on the radio but gathered it was a steam train. When she sees it's only a comedian and not even a Super Sprinter she retreats hastily.

I approach the only man on the station. Is he a train spotter? Yes, he is. He has the notebook and the binoculars. He guides me through the train spotting books the director has bought me; I get quite excited and write down one number. He looks it up and tells me it is a Crewe Electric. It seems a pity this was never the name of a band in 1979. John the spotter tells me he worked on the railways but took voluntary redundancy because his take-home pay was only £95 a week, but if he worked a twelve-hour shift on a Sunday he could bump it up to £125. 'Fortunately I'm not married.' He lives with his twin brother, who appears, eating chips and not looking much like a twin. 'He doesn't smoke or drink – might as well be a nun.' Heavy chip bill, though, I gather.

We reach Glasgow: hooray, a proper station, old and new mixed together to make a workable, efficient place that's not lowering to the spirits. At first glance I think it's been olde-worldefied, but it hasn't – they've just done up all the original old bits. I'm sick of the past, and I've never even been there. What's the point of steam trains going three miles back and forth? We all want fast trains to everywhere – that's the only way to get people off the roads. I'm anti-car this week. The pollution in London has made me feel ill – and guilty because I love driving and do it all the time.

I like the Central Hotel. It's not too posh or too 'authentic'. I have a suite of rooms, all huge, but it's not been too Edwardianized. In fact the decor has a nice eighties feel, a decade as yet overlooked by the nostalgic. I have tea in a lounge crammed with old ladies, all hale and hearty, hoovering up the mixed biscuits and downing huge pots of tea. I ask for Earl Grey. Ina brings it: 'It's Darjeeling.' I just go, 'Oh, OK', instead of taking up the matter immediately in the way advised by consumer watchdogs. ('What the hell do you mean by this, Ina? Fetch the manager, this is an outrage . . .')

A lone man enters – he doesn't even have a custard cream, he's off. The three ladies nearest me decide the sun is over the yardarm, or over John Menzies, and break out into three halves of lager and light up. Speaking of fags, I meet a chauffeur who tells me about Danny Kaye playing the notorious Glasgow Empire. At the height of his popularity in the UK, he was disconcerted when walking on stage to find he wasn't greeted with any applause.

OVERLEAF **At Grange-over-Sands the station windows look out over Morecambe Bay**

Rattled, he asked one of the band for a fag, lit up and smoked it. That got the audience going and he went really well. What an act, eh? None of this sweating over two hours of finely honed comic material – just twenty Bensons and a box of Swan Vestas and they'd be begging for more. No wonder the bloody theatres were always burning down.

We spend half the night in the Central Hotel and then get up at 3.30 to catch the Fort William sleeper at Dalmuir Station in the suburbs of Glasgow. Me being compulsive, I have to get up at 2.30 and sit staring at an Infomercial for an exercise bike that, quite frankly, if it came to our house, would stay in its box. Even the people paid to sing its praises don't look too keen. The video that accompanies it shows a thrilling routine consisting of getting off the bike, waving your arms and getting back on – unless they are semaphoring, 'Help, I'm trapped in Infomercial World. I'm condemned to slice tomatoes in fancy patterns and set fire to my car's paintwork for ever. Please contact Amnesty.'

On the Fort William sleeper I am reading a thriller by Josephine Tey, all about a man who is found murdered on the Fort William sleeper. I check the cubicle. I can barely fit in myself, there's certainly no room for assailants. The sleeping car attendant is assiduous, to say the least. *When* will I be having my croissant and juice, *where* do I want them? Every time I go out for a wander I have to call him to let me back in and there are more urgent queries about juice and croissants. If it's a Scottish croissant it'll probably be deep fried anyway. I become so reluctant to talk to this attendant that the next time I go to the loo I wedge the door open with a bag, hoping that no Tey fan will nip in and plant a bit of false evidence.

It's a lovely way to travel, sitting up in bed, scenery whizzing by, and how brilliant to go to bed at horrible Euston (in filthy London) and wake up in Fort William. I talk to two members (possibly the only two) of STORM. This stands for Stop This Railway Madness – not a perfect acronym. I prefer TARTAN (Try And Repeal This Asinine Naffery) and TATTIES (Try And Thwart This Insane Economic System). They are worried that, once the railways are privatized, the Scottish service will be deliberately run down and reduced to some infrequent shuttle between tartan exhibitions and haggis bars.

Fort William is full of frighteningly energetic sixty-year-old couples, the men scrutinizing steam engines and the women looking pityingly on and holding thermoses. I have one myself, and a Mickey Mouse lunchbox, thirty years too late to impress my friends at school.

We have brek (promised croissants never arrived) at the foot of Ben Nevis at a walkers' café. I get a bunch of bananas at a caravan site shop and am as happy as a bee eating them and staring up at the sunny mountainside. We gawp admiringly until our driver tells us scathingly, 'They push beds up it for charity. It's the other side that's dangerous.'

We get the steam train to Mallaig, on the edge of the Hebrides. No real nostalgia here – the coaches are like the ones from the Bury-to-Manchester line in the mid-sixties, passing through Radcliffe and Besses O' The Barn. I feel like I'm off for a day's shopping in Deansgate or Market Street, hunting down an egg-yellow PVC coat-dress at C & A's department store.

Mallaig is all cafés and gift shops. Everywhere smells of diesel now. Is it the ferries or have I got pollution up my nose? We walk out of a pub because, although they do eggs and they do chips, they won't do egg and chips. I realize they are not naturally hospitable when I ask, 'Have you got a phone?' to be told 'Yes.' Well, don't tell me where it is, you ARSE!

We take the ferry to Skye. The driver (pilot? master?) calls me Julie Walters. I die laughing. He is still doing it twenty minutes after I have walked away. In fact I leave Scotland altogether and he's still at it.

I take a trip round Skye on a post bus (there aren't any trains on the island). There is a terrible SMELL. It could well be me, or it could be a previous passenger who'd missed a deodorant delivery. The postman who's driving doesn't like being filmed and answers even simple questions like 'What's your name?' with 'Oh God, I'm sorry.' I should have cut my losses and interviewed the BO. I go back over to The Kyle of Lochalsh, which is very pretty with ferries going back and forth to Skye. It seems to me that the romantic view is somewhat spoiled by the new causeway, but I don't know any of the political ins and outs and anyway I have a train to catch.

We get off the Inverness train at Dingwall, which, like Kyle, has a proper teashop with tablecloths and local gifts for sale. I think every station should do this – much more interesting than old Knickerbox and Sock Shop wherever you go. We have a three-hour wait for our train, and we hoik all our equipment over the latticework bridge (or, as we're in Scotland, perhaps I mean Hawick).

ABOVE Victoria Wood catches a quick nap while waiting for a
connection at Dingwall in the Highlands

OPPOSITE At Kyle of Lochalsh the traditional ferries from the
mainland to the Isle of Skye were replaced in 1995 by a
controversial new road bridge

Our minder from Scotrail rips his trousers on said bridge and gives us all a flash of bright turquoise underpants, nothing to be ashamed of. He pins it all together with a Scotrail medal and stops blushing.

Helmsdale, further north, is our next stop. It's a little grey fishing village, the focal point of which, for us at least, is La Mirage, a bright pink café full of parasols, plastic fruit and signed photos of Phil Collins. Actually I notice another photo of Phil in a rival establishment across the road. He's very free with his favours, obviously – an egg and chips here, a ham salad bap there. I'm only jealous. Nancy at La Mirage has done me ratatouille specially, because I'm a vegetarian, so once again I'm thwarted in my desire for egg and chips. Nancy is big and blonde and veering more towards the Dusty Springfield than the Norma Major cosmetics-wise, and if she does you ratatouille specially you have it.

I'm shown round the Timespan Visitor Centre, which displays scenes of Scottish rural life – not a bundle of laughs, being burnt at the stake and cleared off the land by eighteenth-century English toffs. There is a pink niche dedicated to Barbara Cartland, not the first name to spring to mind when brooding on the Highland Clearances, but it appears she has some sort of hunting lodge up the road. I like to think of her in a lavender Puffa, rifle cocked ready to pick off a brace of minor romantic novelists.

The train to Thurso takes us past acres of moorland and I look out for eagles and wild boar, but no luck. The guard tells me deer are often killed by running on to the track (can't they read?) and I check the refreshment trolley anxiously. But it's only the usual Kit-Kat bars and egg sandwiches – no venison and tomato baps. In Thurso, overlooking the Orkneys, people look Scottish at last – sandy hair and freckles and lots of Anguses. I nip to the Co-op for bananas. The woman at the check-out serving the customer ahead of me suddenly goes away with no change of expression. She's like someone in a science fiction movie who has been programmed to kill when they hear the word 'onions'. She comes back with twenty Players. I board the train with my bananas and head south.

Travelling back south to Edinburgh we take a slight detour to look at the underside of the Forth Bridge, which reminds me of lots of old jokes about Queen Mary's bottom. We go in a boat and, as we embark, we see a film crew from Sky TV. Or perhaps it is Skye TV. In fact, wherever we go we follow film crews or talk to people who have already done three interviews that morning. Little old ladies say to us, 'I see this as a close two-shot with a cut-away mixing to a wide.' The deal on the Forth Bridge is this: some people think it is not being maintained to its former standard because of safety regulations, and is becoming dangerously rusty. And some people think it was over-engineered originally and needs no more than a wipe with a damp cloth once every twenty years. This sounds like a job for Vicky, Girl Reporter.

I meet Mary, who lives as close to actually underneath the bridge as you'd want to go, unless you were sexually attracted to rivets. She produces an impressively large cardboard box full of huge bits of ironmongery and bolts which she has collected from near her house. Asked what actually fell in her garden, she brings out a small margarine tub containing medium-size flakes of rust. She reckons if they don't slap a few more coats of paint on sharpish, the residents of North Queensferry will be ducking shrapnel daily and will need air-raid shelters and a visit from Vera Lynn. In the interests of balanced reporting we accept a bolt and go in search of the other side of the story.

At Dalmeny Station, which is very pretty and has beautiful flower beds and window boxes, I talk to an engineer who is very scathing about this idea that they have stopped painting the bridge. He says they never did paint all of it from end to end (that was a bit of a disappointment to me), but only paint the bits that need doing. I am equally convinced by him and can see I'll never make it in investigative journalism.

We cross the bridge by train, and I decide it looks both completely safe and dangerously crumbly. Our lady minder from Railtrack gives me a souvenir rivet, and remarks that it reminds her of a penis. This worries me for her social life. Is it full of male friends daubing their genitalia with red rustproof pigment? I thought that only went on in English public schools. (I must say, however, that we do get a bit of stick at Manchester airport when that rivet shows up on the X-ray machine in the director's hand luggage.)

We change trains at Edinburgh for Newcastle and I have time for a bit of shopping. I manage to purchase a Scottie dog tea-towel, a tartan dinosaur

OVERLEAF **Inland from Helmsdale the train passes through rolling green countryside**

and a CD of Andy Stewart. I happen to believe his interpretation of 'Donald Where's Your Trousers' is a landmark in popular post-war culture. One of our crew says she is looking for 'a suitable boy'. Fortunately I realize in time she means that book by Vikram Seth, and that I am not being asked to produce a list of affable bachelors.

Edinburgh to Newcastle is a lovely journey with lots of sea views, and it's sunny today as well. We change at Newcastle for Middlesbrough and I nod off over my Angus Wilson novel. When I wake up, the woman opposite me has sprouted a mole under her chin. Either reading Angus Wilson has sharpened my powers of observation or it's a free gift with her *People's Friend* magazine and she'll take it off at bedtime.

The Middlesbrough-to-Glaisdale run begins in a thick grey mist, but halfway through the journey the sun comes out and it all begins to look wonderful. I could just do this all day: going up and down the line looking out at tiny stations, men carrying geese, dog roses, foxgloves, hawthorn and fields of cows. There's nothing modern to be seen, and I feel I have slipped into the world of H. G. Wells and E. Nesbit. Where is my straw boater and my tweed cycling costume? I want a lemonade bottle with a stone stopper and a sixpenny ham tea in a fat woman's garden. Glaisdale doesn't break the spell: I'm looking out for the Railway Children with a pram full of birthday presents for Perks. Even a quiet road is sometimes noisy, but a railway track between trains is silent. What a filthy old world it is, and what a lovely place to take a breather.

I talk to a man who in the days of steam worked his way up to fireman from the lowly position of knocker-up of engine drivers. But his fiancée lived miles away in Middlesbrough and he found the shift system interfered with his courting, so he packed in the railways and got a job maintaining beer pumps. He is very funny about train spotters and says when he was in the cab he used to cover up the engine number with his cap just to annoy them. He lets slip he's on his way to Whitby to swim in the sea. I ask him if he's one of those barmy people who takes a dip on Christmas Day, he proudly says he is. He swims every week in Sutton Park. Isn't the water filthy? I ask. That's the best bit, he says. 'It spoils it if you have a wash.'

On the platform at Glaisdale Nigel is waiting to take his goat on the train. He reckons it's some unrepealed railway bye-law that lets him do it. I think it's a put-up job. The goat wees all the time and someone is quite likely to take a header into the sleepers if they're not careful. Nigel is actually rather sweet. His mother was the signalwoman and they both lived on the station in what is now a very tasteful teashop. Nigel now lives in a caravan that looks like an explosion at a car boot sale. I stand with him in the teashop garden, all rockery plants and statuary. 'When we lived here this was wall-to-wall sheds,' he says sadly. Those were the days.

The next morning I take the 'Hooligan Express' – the school train to Whitby from Glaisdale. In fact the children are very well behaved and three lads are poring over the *War Cry*. At Whitby we have brek at an Indian restaurant on the station, but I am not in poppadom mood and go out in search of rock. The place seems very big on rock and I pick up rock bacon'n'eggs, cigarettes and dentures with no trouble at all. At Whitby I find yet more evidence of the British feel for hospitality. Nowty notices abound: 'Don't eat YOUR food on OUR premises', 'You don't like your breakages, neither do we', 'Twenty pounds reward for naming the cowardly moron who stole this chalkboard.'

We drive to Grosmont and take the steam train to Pickering. This train has a lovely 1930s Art Deco buffet bar, very unpopular with the nostalgia buffs because it doesn't conform to the toffee-varnish-red-plush idea of the steam era. This is all so artificial – trains that never ran on this line, running for no other reason than that they no longer do so.

We break our journey at Goathland, which is where they film the hugely popular sixties TV police serial *Heartbeat*. All the gift shops have souvenirs sporting the face of its star, Nick Berry, but, alas, the woolly doll I have my eye on is not for sale. Shame: a knitted Nick makes a natty knick-knack.

In the buffet, I engage two American tourists in conversation. He thinks he has seen me before and asks me if I am famous. 'Yes,' I say boldly. 'Oh yes,' he recalls, 'we saw you on TV last night. You were hilarious.' His wife adopts the unconvincing cheeriness of a member of the royal family meeting a drug addict. 'We laughed a lot,' she murmurs and stares firmly out of the window. Unfortunately at that point we are passing a white bottle bank on which someone has spray-painted a penis. I don't apologize; if it was in a Minoan cave everyone would think it was bloody marvellous.

ABOVE Railway workers from the Esk Valley Line at Grosmont in
North Yorkshire down a welcome pint or two

OPPOSITE Steaming out of Grosmont on the way to Pickering

We take the bus to Malton. Here I find my best railway buffet so far, though the little stone station is rather overshadowed by a new Kwiksave. The clientele are mainly elderly, on their way to York or Scarborough. They sit discussing *Heartbeat* and Nick Berry, and I stick a giant rock fag in the ashtray but no one notices. There are Wagon Wheels and Eccles cakes on the counter and a gas fire. It has not been done up or preserved. I'm sick of nostalgia; I want to go home. (Joke.)

York is polluted and fuggy, and the gift shops are full of such famous York characters as Winnie the Pooh and Peter Rabbit. I go into an antique shop to ask the price of a 1930 Clarice Cliff ceramic jug. The woman behind the counter recoils. 'It's hardly a jug – it's a ewer!' I nearly buy it out of spite. I look round for the inevitable notice: 'We don't ask the price of YOUR jugs, don't ask the price of OURS.'

At York Railway Museum they let me sit in one of the royal trains, Queen Mary's. It's tasteful and rather dull, though the bathroom is rather dinky, with the window frosted on the platform side, just in case (we're back to Queen Mary's bottom again). The curtains are faded and the nets are grey; it's obvious to me old Mary wasn't exactly a dab hand with the soap powder.

We whizz along away from York back towards Manchester. The scenery isn't very spectacular but the train is excellent – brand-new, comfortable and very clean. I really do think that when it's good it's the best way to travel; but at its worst, it's depressing and irritating. People seem exposed on the platforms. Away from our cars, we've forgotten how to be in a crowd.

We visit a man who collects engines and puts them in his back garden. He bought the plot as soon as it came on the market, irrespective of what house would be built there. Like most of the railway enthusiasts I've met he is intelligent and articulate, though I can't really follow him down this track. The engines are squashed together on concrete; unrestored and rusty, they lack the cosification factor – they are pure railway, with nothing of the *Brief Encounter* feel about them. I like his enormous 'CARNFORTH' sign, though. He says people ask him if it comes from Carnforth.

We end up back at Crewe, in the buffet. This is my worst one, I think. It has all the ghastliness associated with everyday rail travel. The buttock-resistant vinyl banquettes, the plastic chairs pointlessly grained to resemble woodgrain Formica, the artificial plants, the stupid bloody bunting. All that's missing is a few notices: 'Please spill lager on the beer mats and tear them into small fragments'; 'If you have to cough make sure everyone can hear you, and next time why not gob into the ashtray?'; 'Before boarding your train, please don't forget to smack your child and ram his buggy into someone's ankles.'

I slink off to the Ladies, which is, as most of them have been, slightly grubby and dispiriting but without being bad enough to complain. Perhaps their cleaners are given a check-list to ensure standardization throughout the rail network. Lavatories: clean three, spill water in two others and block the rest by putting a mop and bucket in the way. Basins: wipe desultorily and then decorate using the two long ginger hairs and the grubby cotton wool ball provided.

The lavs on the trains haven't been particularly inspiring, either. Never mind reduced fares for students, they should knock a few bob off the ticket price to anyone who's prepared to nip in and buff up the taps. It would help, too, if they reinstated that notice: 'Gentlemen please lift the seat'. Gents just aren't lifting. You go over rattly points mid-bladder evacuation and it could go anywhere. You could have the St Valentine's Day Massacre all over again.

But Crewe Ladies does have a thrilling piece of graffiti: 'I kissed Zammo from Grange Hill years ago.' I whip out a nailfile and hastily scratch: 'Fancy that, my ex-flatmate once worked with Petula Clark' and then I go and catch my train home.

Across Canada: Halifax to Vancouver

CHRIS BONINGTON

T HE FAÇADE WAS SUBDUED but grand, a touch of classical and Georgian, with its pale grey columns and two embosseed Romanesque figures, one clutching a railway engine and the other a ship, standing above the portal. This was the start of my journey across Canada from Halifax Station on the eastern coast. It was tucked into an even bigger and more imposing building that had recently been the station hotel, but this seemed to be in mothballs, cocooned by contractors' partition walls with a skeleton of scaffolding clinging to its front. It was being converted, I was told, into apartments. There was no line of taxis, no people bustling in and out of the doors of the station.

I pushed the door open to walk into an empty, airy hall. It was clean and tidy, as if just abandoned, a *Mary Celeste* of the Canadian Railways. It was not so much like a railway station as a rather sparse conservatory with its chequered tiled floor, pot plants and container-grown trees. On one side was a glassed-in ticket booth, and to my relief I could just discern someone part-hidden by a computer.

'I've come to collect my tickets,' I said. 'Name of Bonington. I'm going all the way to Vancouver.'

Ready for anything: Chris Bonington climbs aboard at Halifax, Nova Scotia

He keyed my name into the computer and eventually there spewed forth page after page of ticketing to take me all the way across Canada. It even had a folder very similar to the ones that hold airline tickets.

'Not many people around,' I observed.

'Only got one train a day, and that's not till two this afternoon. It'll get busy around lunchtime.'

I was to discover that this was a reflection of what has happened to Canada's railways. When I was invited to take part in the *Great Railway Journeys* series I was immediately attracted to the concept of crossing this huge country. I had memories from previous flights to the west coast of America of hour after hour crossing northern Canada at 10 000 metres, and looking down in summer at the dark green of endless forests broken by the sheen of myriad lakes and serpentine rivers, while in winter I stared out at the almost black of the forest in contrast to the startling white of endless snows. There were no roads, no straight lines, none of the scars of development or people that are visible even when flying over the deserts of Asia or Siberia. It was just a gigantic emptiness that I found immensely appealing.

But this opportunity was different. It meant crossing the continent by that comparatively narrow band of populated land that clings to the US border, squeezed between the wilderness and the richest, most powerful, most highly developed country in the world. And now here I was in Halifax, about to start that journey.

I was already discovering that the state of the Canadian railways was very different from the days when immigrants arriving by boat in Halifax could travel in the same train to Vancouver, 2750 miles away, in five and a half days. The building of railways had played a vital part in the formation of the country. Nova Scotia and Newfoundland had only agreed to join Canada in 1867 on the promise of a rail link with Montreal. British Columbia had been coaxed into the nation with the same promise in 1871. The building of the Canadian Pacific Railway, which was completed in 1885, not only helped to unite Canada but was one of the most remarkable engineering feats in the history of railways throughout the world. But it is very different today. The last daily passenger service from Halifax to Vancouver ran in 1990. Hundreds of miles of branch lines have been closed and passenger services have almost vanished.

The distances between cities are so great it is easier to fly, and for shorter distances the low price of petrol and the supremacy of the car have killed all too many commuter lines. Freight, on the other hand, is highly profitable and even expanding. Huge trains driven by just two engineers can haul 12000 tonnes from one side of Canada to the other. The big container docks and freight sidings at Halifax were witness to this.

So this steel lifeline was now reduced, as far as passengers were concerned, to a tourist line running once daily between Halifax and Montreal, and further west from Toronto to Vancouver just three times a week. Montreal and Toronto are linked by several express trains per day, a genuine working passenger service still used by business people and travellers. I was to be a tourist, so at least I could take my time and spend a few days in Halifax before the start of my odyssey.

I hired a mountain bike so that I could ride around the city itself and also explore outside it. Only a few weeks earlier it had hosted the summit meeting of the seven leading trading nations of the world, perhaps an effort by Canada to raise the profile and morale of what seems in danger of becoming an economic and political backwater. The summit had doubtless brought back memories of busier times when during two world wars Halifax had been the starting place of the convoys that maintained Britain's lifeline with the American continent. The city never experienced a direct attack but in 1917 a French ship carrying munitions collided with another boat, detonating its volatile cargo and leading to the biggest single explosion the world had ever seen. Half of Halifax was flattened and two thousand people lost their lives.

Today, even though it is the largest city in Canada east of Montreal, with a population of 300000, it has a sleepy feel. The high rises are not too high, the suburbs with their roads of pleasant clapboard buildings nudge closely into the centre, and the age of the city – one of the oldest in Canada – is reflected with a profusion of mansions of solid granite blocks reminiscent of Aberdeen. But what struck me most of all was the courtesy I encountered, both when I asked the way and also on the roads as I cycled.

I had arrived on Saturday, 1 July, just in time for Canada Day. The local festivities centred on the Citadel and I looked forward to immersing myself in Canadian nostalgia. I have always been fascinated by fortifications and as a teenager, just before I discovered climbing, had spent my holidays cycling from castle to castle exploring their ramparts and dreaming of battles fought long ago. The Citadel was no medieval fortification with crenellated towers and ramparts, but a fortress of the nineteenth century designed to withstand artillery bombardment. Inside was a spacious parade ground and a barracks that housed its garrison. Soldiers in full nineteenth-century uniform were marching up and down performing the drill movements of the period, while a kilted Highland infantryman stood on guard over the main gate. It was a step back in time, all the more intriguing when I discovered that these were not soldiers re-enacting the past, but professional re-enactors who were taken on for the season to march and drill for the benefit of the tourists.

A ferocious pseudo-NCO brought back memories of my own basic training as he screamed at a hapless soldier who was out of step with the rest. A closer look showed me that it was a woman who was being yelled at. The government, strong on equal opportunities, had insisted that women should be eligible to serve in this nineteenth-century army.

The original garrison had all been British and had often come from Highland regiments. The mournful skirl of pipes from a solitary piper seemed particularly appropriate on this wet, drizzling, grey day that was so similar to many I have experienced in the Highlands. Jack MacLean, the pipe major, certainly looked the part – tall, with a deep chest and fine girth, and a neatly trimmed beard and moustache – in his Highland green and tartan kilt. His bagpipes were a new pair which he had purchased for several hundred dollars by mail order from Edinburgh. He had been working as a re-enactor for the last five years during the season, doing a bit of teaching and taking on odd jobs over the winter. It was just a job, but at the same time it enabled him to work as a musician.

It was time for the midday gun to be fired. The dark blue uniformed artillery people with their neat little pillbox hats marched in step carrying the tools of their trade, buckets, swabs and ramrods, to the muzzle-loading cannon that fired daily. It was followed by a modern-day salute by a troop of three howitzers from the real Canadian Army. It was as stylized as the drill of the

Pipe Major Jack MacLean, resplendent in tartan at the Citadel in Halifax

SIGNAL. POST

make-believe soldiers, and once again both sexes were represented. I was surprised by how emotionally moving I found the ceremony: the roar of the guns, the jets of smoke in the rain-soaked air, the marionette-like movement of the crews, all set against the grey backdrop of the high-rise buildings of Halifax partly obscured by the low cloud, with the river behind and the great leap of the suspension bridge disappearing into the mists.

By this time it was raining heavily and the crowd had thinned considerably. A band had been playing, a choir had sung and now the politicians made their Canada Day speeches to the few sturdy enough to remain before most of the rest of the programme was cancelled. I had enjoyed this introduction to Canadian pageantry. There was something friendly, informal and yet very efficient about it, and even the small crowds on this miserable day reflected the great diversity of people who make up this huge but lightly populated country. I was standing behind a little group of obviously Middle Eastern origin, while nearby there was a group of Amish people; the women wore long skirts and bonnets, while the menfolk were in shirtsleeves and braces. The Scots links with Halifax were evident everywhere, both in place and personal names and also the following day in the Highland games held in the local park.

But it was time to start my journey. With an hour to go to departure for Halifax's only train there was almost a bustle around the station, with a few taxis disgorging passengers and a handful of people in the booking hall. The train itself was like a long fat aluminium millipede, both broader and taller than British trains, with two diesel locomotives out in front, one to pull the train and the other to run the electric lighting and air conditioning, though the latter could also be used to give extra traction if necessary.

Clutching my voluminous ticket, I found Coach 26 and was led to compartment D. It was more stark than I had expected – a little square box with grey walls and carpet, containing two folding chairs. Closer inspection revealed a washbasin set into one wall, a rather insipid framed picture and my own little loo. My bed presumably folded out from the back wall. I dumped my bags and went off to explore.

I was next door to the restaurant car, which was pleasantly spacious and open – as was the whole train. At the very back was the observation car with a little bar, self-service coffee and seats arranged around the side, facing inwards. It was an invitation for people to talk to each other. From here a small staircase went up to an observation deck in the roof. Light and airy, with glass all round, it gave a superb view both of the passing countryside and of the train itself.

As we pulled slowly out of the station we rolled past train after train stacked with containers from the port. Halifax slipped away quickly and the ubiquitous forest closed in on either side of the track, allowing the occasional glimpse of houses or cleared fields. I started chatting to the man in the seat in front of me. Peter Butler was a professor of social sciences and anthropology at the University of Halifax. He was travelling with his teenage son to Montreal to pick up an imported car, a BMW, and had chosen the train to make it a small holiday trip. Sharp and incisive, he was an expert on polling and obviously had a thriving private practice in this field. He had even been brought over to Britain in 1988 to advise Margaret Thatcher. Presumably he got it right.

I have always been interested in politics, and one of the attractions of this journey was the opportunity to look at this huge, diverse country with its many challenges – the question of identity, the overpowering presence of the United States, the issue of Quebec separatism and the growing and more assertive aspirations of the native population. I asked Peter what he thought would happen if Quebec voted for independence from Canada. He didn't think it would ever come to that, a reply I got throughout my journey, even when passing through French Canada, but if it did come about he thought that the eastern provinces would be attracted to the United States – if, of course, the United States would have them. The people of these parts, even though predominantly of Anglo-Saxon origin, felt little in common with central and western Canada, perhaps resenting their more expansive economies. I had liked the feel of the eastern seaboard but at the same time had sensed a disillusionment that was confirmed by Peter Butler.

It was time for a beer as we rolled through the forests of Nova Scotia. At the bar I sat next to a striking couple who were folk singers from Victoria,

OVERLEAF Glass walls and ceiling provide a magnificent observation deck as the train starts to roll west

near the tip of Vancouver Island. Susan and Robert had been on a working holiday, appreciating the leisure of the train to take them to a few singing engagements on the east coast. Robert worked as a freelance quantity surveyor to help support their singing. He produced a guitar and in the gathering dusk they sang homely duets about household events like making blackberry jam. I was going to enjoy this trip and was encouraged by their gentle optimism. They liked being Canadians and hoped the Québecois would want to remain part of Canada.

After dinner I returned to my sleeper to find that the bunk had been dropped down and the bed made. My little box seemed more homely as I snuggled down to sleep, rocked by the motion of the train and the clunkety-clunk of the wheels. I had set my alarm for four in the morning to get an early glimpse of Quebec City. In due course I found myself gazing across the St Lawrence River at its dramatic skyline that at the same time is something of an illusion, for it is dominated by the turreted mass of the Château Frontenac Hotel. This looks like a magnificent seventeenth-century citadel but was in fact built in 1892, a flamboyant affirmation of the importance and wealth of the Canadian Pacific Railway, most of whose hotels of this period were built in the French château style.

In a dawn similar to this, 236 years ago, a flotilla of boats had slipped up the St Lawrence to disembark a British army led by General Wolfe on the northern shore below the Heights of Abraham. They had scaled the steep slopes above the river to surprise the French under General Montcalm and cut him off from his supply base at Montreal. Montcalm had had no choice but to fight the British force, whose superior discipline and murderous volley fire overcame the French, and the resulting victory marked the end of French dominance in Canada. Montreal was captured the following year and, in the peace treaty that ended the Seven Years' War, France ceded Canada to Britain. The British were wise in victory and from the start respected both the French language and religion.

I should have enjoyed wandering round the narrow old streets of Quebec, the focal point of the French identity and culture that have enriched and divided Canada ever since, but soon the train was passing through cultivated fields broken by woodland, with colourful houses and barns. This was the heartland of Canada. Montreal arrived like a space-age fantasy city, the towering skyscrapers of its centre jutting in multi-coloured sculptures of glass and steel, the most aesthetically pleasing modern architecture that I had seen in my travels around America.

But I was going to escape from the city and take to the road to visit a beaver lake in the hills about 100 miles north-west of Montreal. What a contrast; I was standing by a lake created by a dam, an untidy barrage of logs and branches bonded by mud a good 6 feet high. It was difficult to believe that this considerable structure had been built by a family of beavers. The beaver lodge, another untidy pile of branches, was at the other end of the lake. The entrances to the home were all under water, whilst the living chambers were just above water level in the heart of the pile.

I was with Denis Beaudry, a local trapper who spoke only French. He had sad downcast eyes and a drooping moustache, offset by a Gallic charm which he directed at Jill, my interpreter. He talked with enthusiasm, sympathy, indeed almost love, of these determined little animals, whom he also trapped for their furs. It is the eternal contradiction or dilemma of the hunter. Son of a trapper, Denis had been born into this way of life, had first gone out with his father at the age of seven and had left school when only twelve, something that he now regrets. He had inherited his father's territory, but it was difficult to make a living from it and he had pursued a range of other jobs, including logging and working as caretaker of a school in the city. But in spite of the steady pay and regular hours he couldn't stand it, and had returned to the wild. He was now both trapper and conservationist. His task was to ensure that a good balance of moose, beaver and other wildlife was maintained in his territory, and he spent as much time showing groups of tourists and schoolchildren the wonders of the wild as he did hunting.

We went back at dusk to watch the beavers coming out to inspect their dam. The mosquitoes were out in force, gathering in dense clouds around us. Our patience was rewarded when two dark shapes slipped through the water towards me. One of the beavers stood off, obviously on guard, its head protruding from the water, gazing around to detect any threat. The other was pushing a small branch, its tail slapping the water, forming a wake behind it. I could see its protuberant front teeth clamped on to the wood in a grin. It

A beaver lodge, composed of thousands of twigs and small branches, is the result of many hours of patient industry

paddled to the edge of the dam, pushed the twig alongside it and dived back under the water to reappear a few metres out, paddling back to the edge to pick up another stick. There was a feeling of purposeful industry and total focus in the quiet of the night. The only sound was the flap of beaver tails on the water and the distant croak of a bullfrog. Even the mosquitoes were silent.

As I watched the dam-builders I talked with Denis about the question of Quebec independence. He was cautious about what he said, but commented on how much we could learn from the way the beavers conducted their lives and how nature balanced itself out.

The next day we were back in the bustle of Montreal having breakfast in the commercial centre, in Ben's Diner. At first glance an ordinary cheap café with Formica tables, tubular metal chairs and lots of plastic, it is arguably Montreal's most famous eating-place and certainly its best-known deli. The signed photographs around the walls include politicians, musicians, pop stars and pro ice hockey players – a picture of Liberace had pride of place. A small frail man in his eighties had greeted me. This was Al, son of Ben, who still took an active interest in the family business, chatting to customers and making a fuss of the children. His father, an immigrant from Lithuania, had opened the first diner further down the block in 1908.

Although Montreal is a bustling business city it had a laid-back feel, particularly down by the old dock area which had been turned into a park full of avant-garde but pleasing sculpture. Rollerbladers in full gear cruised and swirled down the wide boulevard. A busker with his own amplifier played the electric guitar, and people dozed on the grass in the hot sun. That night I ate outside on the pavement at a bistro in the Rue St Denis, the bohemian quarter. We could easily have been in Paris. The food was every bit as good, but, being Canada, in huge quantities.

Next morning I was on the early commuter train to Toronto. Its station is the grandest of all the Canadian rail terminals, with a main hall like a classical temple to the gods of steam and steel. From here I was to make my way by train to Moosonee at the southern end of James Bay, itself at the bottom end of the vast Hudson Bay. This diversion from the coast-to-coast route would give me an opportunity to look at up-country Ontario. Until 1932 the only contact with Moosonee was by canoe, or in the summer months by boat through Hudson Bay, and only when the railway was pushed through did this little outpost get reliable communications with the outside world. Today there are still no road links, though there is a small airport. During the summer there is a tourist train, the Polar Bear Express, but I was going via Cochrane in northern Ontario where I would catch the Little Bear, a combined passenger and freight train that runs daily all year round.

Cochrane has the atmosphere of a frontier town with wide, empty streets, a couple of run-down clapboard hotels and the dark conifers of the forest on every side. The railway station, a neat red-brick building, doubles as a hotel. With a maximum of two trains a day, it has a sleepy feel.

Preparation for the Little Bear built up to a gentle crescendo during the morning. A church group from Niagara were loading boxes of electrical equipment and pieces of furniture for a church they were planning to open in

OVERLEAF **The area by the old docks in Montreal is now a rollerbladers' paradise**

Moose Factory, the original settlement on an island off Moosonee. Peter, who worked for the Canadian National Park Service, was putting on board a collection of antique chairs, children's toys and kitchen utensils. He was leaving his wife and young child in southern Ontario for the summer while he returned to work.

The train was due to start at ten and eased out of the station around eleven. No one seemed too bothered. Hauled by two locomotives, it rattled and bumped along at little more than 30 mph. The compartments, as on all trains in Canada, were commodious but the upholstery was well worn and it all felt a little run-down in a nice way. This was indeed a working train, with children, most of them Cree Indian, running up and down the aisles while their parents sprawled across the seats and slept through the journey.

A short belt of cultivated land quickly gave way to a forest screen on either side of the line. It could have been of any density – 100 metres or 100 miles look the same – and it gave me claustrophobia. There were no distant hills, no sweeping vistas, just the occasional glimpse of tumbling water over rocks as the train crossed a river. You needed to focus more closely at the detail of shape and texture of the dark spruce, the fragile birch, the bright yellow greens of sphagnum moss, the white of sedge, the sprays of tamarisk and the patterns of dark water in the bog from which the forest grew. We were crossing one of the largest wetlands in the world, a pathless wilderness where only hunters or trappers wandered. Before the Europeans arrived this had been the domain of the Cree Indians, who had used canoes in the summer and snowshoes in winter to hunt and trap. They still have a few homesteads by the railway, and the train stops on demand.

I was being looked after by Glen Fairey from the railway company, Ontario Northland. A friendly, genial man, with his well-pressed khakis, jaunty felt hat, curly grey hair and bushy moustache he reminded me of a travelling doctor in a Western movie. He had a wealth of stories, and described how he had been taking some journalists to Moosonee when the train stopped to drop off a young Indian girl at a path that disappeared into the forest. 'You can't let her go alone like that!' one of the journalists asserted indignantly, only to have it pointed out how much safer that was than anywhere in Toronto or Montreal.

We crossed the Moose River, 600 metres of trestled bridge over a broad sweep of water, and continued up to Moosonee. The place has a population of around 3500, of which 80 per cent are native and most of the remainder work for the government in education, the high school or local government. The town is built on a grid, the houses scattered and nondescript, the roads wide and empty. There are not many roads outside Moosonee and the cars or trucks are all brought in by train. A few Indians sat in little groups on street corners, chatting or passing the time. It was a grey, cloudy day with rain in the air, emphasizing the general air of melancholy.

I wanted to visit Moose Factory, so I took a motorized canoe taxi across the mist-racked sound. I was approaching one of the earliest British settlements in Canada, founded in 1673 by the young Hudson Bay Company to open up the fur trade around James Bay. It was the first permanent English-speaking settlement in what was to become Ontario. They were able to offer the Cree guns, cooking pots, beads and even a variety in their diet in the shape of flour and sugar in return for furs. It was to be the start of the insidious change in the balance of power and lifestyle that was to take the First Nation's control of their land forever away from them. It is only today that they are beginning to recover their identity and the rights over those lands.

Moose Factory is divided between the old Hudson Bay Company concession, which still holds most of the buildings associated with the administration, school, hospital, ubiquitous radio station and a clutch of churches, while the northern part of the island is the Indian reserve. The houses are utilitarian and characterless prefabs. I went straight to the Moose Cree Complex, a large drab building which was the social centre of the Cree community. I was to meet Gilbert, a Cree elder and chief. He was a frail old man who had obviously had a stroke, which had impaired his speech but in no way his mind. I had to listen carefully, but he had a quick and lurking sense of humour. Then we were taken by jeep to a tepee where we met Agnes, who has her own business cooking bannocks for the tourists. The canvas tepee was light and airy, and in the middle the bannocks, consisting of dough rolled round a stick, were cooking over the glowing embers of a wood fire. The bannock is more Scottish than Indian in origin – an indication of how quickly the Indians had become dependent on imported foods.

Enjoying Cree hospitality in Agnes's canvas
tepee in Moose Factory

Sitting next to Agnes was Gilbert's cousin Redfurn, a retired minister.
Both had been taken away from home as children and sent to Catholic
boarding schools, an attempt by the government of the time to integrate the
native people into the Canadian way of life. They were not allowed to speak
their own language at any time and were soundly beaten if caught doing so. I
asked them whether they regretted the attempted exorcizing of their cultural
and linguistic background. Cautious in their reply, they simply said that it was
a good way to learn English quickly and obviously did not want to be drawn
into any controversial discussion.

By this time the bannocks were cooked. Agnes took them off their sticks,
wrapped each in baking foil and handed one to me. Without thinking I started
eating, assuming that this was for me and that she would hand the rest out to
the others. I had been munching away for a few minutes when Gilbert gently
commented, 'One of our Indian traditions is to share our food with our
companions.' I blushed in embarrassment at my lack of sensitivity and

hurriedly offered what little was left of my bannock to the others, to be courteously refused.

On our way back to the canoe, Jack, a young Cree who had picked me up from the landing, said that he too had been sent to boarding school and discouraged from speaking his own language. He wanted to see a change and welcomed the increasing assertiveness of the native people and consequent taking over of the management of their schools and affairs.

Back on the mainland three young canoeists were unloading their boats, having canoed from near Cochrane down the Missinaibi River all the way to Moosonee. It had taken them eight days, with rapids and portages on the way, and they hadn't seen a soul during their trip. It immediately caught my imagination: what a superb way to reach Moosonee! They were now going to load their canoes on to the train for the return journey to civilization. I too was on my way back to urban Canada, cheating by flying to Timmins and then to Toronto.

From the wilds of Moosonee I was transported to the luxury of Toronto's Royal York Hotel. Built in 1929, it was then, with 1200 bedrooms, the largest hotel in the British Empire. It has hosted over 40 million guests, contains 72 kilometres of carpeting, 500 kilometres of pipes, uses 10 tonnes of ice cubes every day, recycles 7 tonnes of garbage daily and launders 7 million pieces of linen each year. The corridors are long and a little gloomy, but I had been given a suite which exuded an air of Edwardian opulence.

That night I dined with the chef, George McNeill, in his office at the heart of this huge kitchen which serves thousands of meals a day. The office was walled with windows so that he could keep an eye on what was going on. In one corner was a table laid for two, and George, a tall, neat man clad in immaculate whites with a traditional chef's hat, was waiting for me at his desk. Even though it was just before dinner time, the place seemed amazingly quiet and unhurried. I asked George how he managed his kitchen but he was much more interested in exploring the problems of catering at 8000 metres above sea level and whether I had seen the Yeti. We talked about expedition diets and meals before he excused himself to work on the meal he was personally preparing for me, and no doubt to check out what was being prepared for the rest of his customers.

A waiter poured me a glass of crisp Canadian white wine. Quail was followed by filleted salmon on a bed of fennel and apple salad. The watchful waiter, who looked more like a maître d'hôtel, topped up my glass. It was roast caribou next, the same dark meat as venison but with a richer, more mellow flavour. This was accompanied by a smooth red wine. I was fascinated to know how George managed this huge kitchen with its staff of 128. It was a hierarchic structure which he described as a brigade system with himself the general in absolute command; then came 9 sub-chefs, 9 junior sub-chefs, 18 chefs de partie, various first cooks and second cooks, and apprentices. It was a combination of craft and mass production, with everything having to move in harmony to create the dish ordered by the customer.

The following morning I met up with Adrian Gordon, an old friend of mine who had been with me on two Everest expeditions – the South West Face in 1975 and the North East Ridge in 1982. He had been in the Army in 1975, in one of the Gurkha regiments, and consequently spoke fluent Nepali. On leaving the Army he had settled in Hong Kong, marrying a local Chinese girl called Frenda. Charlie, his young son, was my godson. Concerned about Hong Kong reverting to Chinese rule in 1997, they had emigrated to Canada in the early 1990s. Over lunch we exchanged news. Frenda, tiny, vivacious and bubbling with enthusiasm, has a dazzling smile and an irrepressible optimism. Adrian, on the other hand, seemed a little battered by the last few years. Things hadn't been easy. He had arrived just before the recession, had had business problems and was living on a tight budget. Even though there are so many opportunities in Canada for enjoying the outdoors, they tend to involve travelling long distances, which costs both time and money. As a result it was difficult for the family to escape from their home in Burlington, a town just outside Toronto. Perhaps, I wondered, he might have been better settling in the west, where the mountains and wilderness are much closer.

In many ways it was easier for Frenda. The Hong Kong Chinese community is very strong in Toronto and she had several friends who were already living there when she arrived. She got to know local people through her children's school and when going shopping. To get more qualifications she had gone back to high school to study accountancy, laughing at how hard she was prepared to work compared to her younger fellow students.

Charlie, now eleven, is quiet and self-contained, but articulate and polite. When he arrived in Canada he was about a year ahead of the others in his class. He too had come into a very different culture. Whereas in Hong Kong school life had been very formal and tightly disciplined, and the children had worked hard, his new school was much more relaxed. He'd had a hard time at first, putting up with a great deal of teasing, but he'd come through it and now had plenty of friends and felt very much a Canadian.

I was glad to leave Toronto. The thought of the enormous emptiness of the Canadian west between us and the Rocky Mountains was immensely alluring. Although I had been on my travels for over a week, I was still in eastern Canada. Perhaps I had the same sense of frustration that that small group of far-sighted politicians and entrepreneurs must have had in the 1870s, when they conceived the plan of pushing a railway across the empty prairies and through the huge barrier of the Rockies to British Columbia, thus uniting Canada. At that time the old Canada of the eastern seaboard provinces, French-speaking Quebec and Ontario were linked by rail, but British Columbia was more remote than if it had been separated by sea.

The story of the building of the railway is an epic of political in-fighting, of wild speculation, of greed and corruption and, at the same time, of extraordinary courage and endurance. In the political arena Alexander MacKenzie and Sir John A. MacDonald, the leaders of the Liberal and Conservative parties, battled over the means – though each perceived the vital need to link their huge, empty, infant nation. It was the financier George Stephen who staked his fortune on completing the project, with a single-mindedness that was more altruistic than business-like and which very nearly destroyed him. The task of masterminding the construction was given to William van Horne, an American professional railroad builder who became general manager of the Canadian Pacific. His dynamic determination and organizational powers were to overcome the seemingly impossible. The cast of players were colourful, individualistic and forceful, driven by an extraordinary combination of greed, ego and idealism. In every way it was a mammoth task against all the odds.

OVERLEAF **Six engines pulling a freight train between Calgary and Banff**

105

First they had to blast their way through the unforgiving granite of the Cambrian Shield, the belt of ice-polished rock only just below the top soil that runs across Canada from north of the Great Lakes all the way to Nova Scotia. It comes down to the very shores of Lake Superior, creating a barrier as formidable as that presented by the Rocky Mountains. This obstacle was so challenging that it was left until the end, and right up to the last moment there were thoughts of taking the easier route south of the Great Lakes and through the United States. Then there were the miles of empty prairie across which the railway builders pushed at breakneck speed, sometimes running out up to 5 miles of track per day, before meeting the final barrier of the Rockies. The whole thing was run like a gigantic military operation. The surveyors went first, marking out the route; then came the graders, towed by teams of horses, creating the embankment on which the rails were to be placed; finally it was the turn of the track layers, manhandling the ties, then running out the rails and hammering them in place. It was an exercise in precision drill and, as with an army, its success largely depended on the flow of supplies brought up by train that fed and housed the workers and provided everything that was necessary to keep this prodigious enterprise going.

It was difficult to imagine that early struggle as I sat in the elegant restaurant car of the Canadian, traditionally the flagship of the Canadian Pacific and now the one remaining passenger train making the through journey form Toronto to Vancouver. I sipped a glass of Canadian red wine and tucked into a Chateaubriand steak as I gazed out at the prairie in the golden glow of a setting sun. It wasn't as empty as I had anticipated. There were more features – little river valleys that curled across the landscape, clusters of trees and shrubs and gentle undulations that caught my imagination.

Having set out from Toronto just after midday, the train reached Saskatoon at 1.30 in the morning two days later. I had had a couple of hours' sleep before stumbling on to the station platform to be taken into town to the old railway hotel. Next morning a handful of people were lining the sidewalk, some of them sitting in folding chairs; they were obviously expecting something. I could hear distant band music, then a police car with flashing lights cruised slowly past followed by a succession of floats, stagecoaches, cars and little groups carrying flags or banners announcing their identity. I asked one of the onlookers what it was all about, to be told that they were celebrating Saskatchewan's ninetieth birthday. There was something very innocent and fresh about it, with the children on the floats or rollerblading in front, the cowboys riding big horses, and members of the Elks sitting in their armchairs waving to the onlookers. They seemed to have a gentle pride in who they were and what they were doing. Just about every company, interest group or service appeared to be represented and it took over an hour to roll, clip-clop and cycle past.

In the afternoon I managed to find a climbing gym. I was definitely getting withdrawal symptoms, since I hadn't been climbing for over a fortnight and was feeling stodgy from too much food and too little exercise. In addition, when we reached the Rockies I had arranged to meet up with Barry Blanchard, one of Canada's best all-round climbers, and I wanted to check out whether I could still climb. Vic's Vertical Climbing Wall was in a run-down industrial estate on the outskirts of Saskatoon. Vic, the owner, who had the stringy build of the modern sports climber, had taken up climbing a few years earlier and had seen the potential for a climbing gym in the city. It was nearly 1000 miles to the nearest rock and as a result most of Vic's clients had never, and were never likely to, touch real rock. There were ropes dangling down each route, giving the security of a top rope, so I chose one that was merely vertical and set off up it. Having climbed it without too much of a struggle, I tried another that Vic said was a bit harder. It was. I was talking too much, lost concentration and fell off – to be held by the rope.

By this time three other climbers, all in their teens, had arrived. One of them, an Asian, had climbed on real rock. The other two had never been outside Vic's wall. But they knew the routes, were strong and supple and were creaming up some of the steep overhanging lines. By this time I'd reached my limit on a series of widely spaced red holds that went over a bulge. It was time to change the topic and I moved on to politics. Did Vic think Quebec would cede?

'Oh it's just a load of politicians that are making all the fuss. I know a lot of French Canadians and I don't think the ordinary guys want to leave Canada, but they do want their own identity and language and I think they've got every right to that.'

TOP On the province of Saskatchewan's ninetieth birthday, the citizens of its capital, Saskatoon, dress up to parade the streets

ABOVE The chuck wagon races at the Calgary Stampede recall the days of the first European settlers

'What about you? How do you feel as a Canadian?'

'I think it's one of the greatest countries in the world to live in. I wouldn't live anywhere else. I've travelled a lot in the States and they seem a more busy people, not quite as relaxed as we are up here. We're a very laid-back culture.' I agreed with that.

Calgary, the next morning, did not seem so laid back. It juts in a cluster of glass, towering above the rolling prairie with the serrated peaks of the Rockies on the skyline behind it. It was packed with visitors for Stampede week, arguably the biggest and most famous rodeo show of the whole West, north or south of the border. I'd never been to a rodeo, but enjoyed dressing up as a cowboy and relished my press pass which enabled me to reach many places closed to the general public.

Mike Mortimer, a climbing store proprietor and expatriate from York-shire, looked after me. A bluff, outspoken character, still very much a Yorkshireman, he was now President of the Canadian Alpine Club. A friend of his, Dixon Thompson, also a climber, has a passion for chuck wagon racing, one of the main events of the Calgary Stampede. Although a professor of environmental science at Calgary University, he looked more like a cowboy than a climber or an academic. He was stocky, with a broad, weatherbeaten face, and wore jeans with a huge silver buckle, a check shirt and a battered felt hat. Some years earlier he had won a ride in a chuck wagon with Doyle Mullaney, a well-known racer, and was now his regular deputy driver. The event is a colourful spectacle, much more fun than ordinary horse racing. In each race there are four teams consisting of a chuck wagon, which is little more than a box on four wheels with four horses to pull it, and four outriders. At the blast of a klaxon the outriders fling a token stove and tent into the back of the wagon. The outrider holding the horses lets go, they lunge forward and the driver has to steer them in a tight figure of eight around some drums that presumably represent the confines of the camp site. This takes them on to the open track and all four teams hurtle down it in a cloud of dust, hotly pursued by their outriders who have had to mount their horses and catch up with their wagon. It's all over in a matter of minutes. Doyle had been having a series of bad runs and was well down the ranking, but this night he was either lucky or inspired, for he came first equal in his heat.

I joined the train early next morning at Calgary Station. Hidden beneath an office block, it hardly resembles a station. The reception area is a cross between a small coach station and an airport, with complimentary tea and coffee machines and seats for the passengers waiting to board the Rocky Mountaineer, a privately owned tour train running through the Rockies to Vancouver. I was taking it as far as Banff, just over an hour's journey from Calgary. On boarding the train, which was painted a rich royal blue, we certainly started on the right note, drinking a toast in champagne to the journey ahead with a little clutch of first-class passengers in the observation car.

The champagne toast was followed by the usual huge breakfast. I sat down with a middle-aged couple.

'Aren't you Chris Bonington?' one of them asked.

'Yes.'

'We went to one of your lectures years ago in Leeds. Are you still climbing?' The tone implied that with my grey beard I must be much too old. I explained that, yes, I still went climbing, had been to the Himalayas earlier in the year and was meeting a friend in Canmore, near Banff, to go climbing. They were on holiday, going to see one of their children who had emigrated to Vancouver, so were travelling by train and then hiring a car to drive back at their leisure. They had very nearly missed the train, having arrived in Calgary from England only the previous evening and then overslept – the train had actually waited ten minutes for them.

As we chatted the hills on either side became bigger, little outliers of woodland joined together to become forest, and the streams and rivers we crossed became streaked with swirls of white as the waters tumbled over the rocks. Beyond, the mountains jutted above the forest in jagged limestone towers and walls. When the train stopped at Banff I set out and drove the few miles back to Canmore, which is just outside the National Park and has become a local climbing centre.

Barry Blanchard, my climbing partner for the day, had pioneered a host of hard routes in the Rockies and had scaled the formidable North Ridge of Rakaposhi, a peak of 7788 metres in the Karakoram range in Pakistan. He made a living as a mountain guide, did a bit of writing and had worked on a series of films, including *Cliff Hanger* in which he had stood in for Sylvester

Stallone in the climbing sequences. With long black hair held back from his eyes by a headband he is of Métis stock, from the French Canadian trappers and American Indians. This proud race has its own customs and traditions and, like the American Indians, had been displaced by the settlers sweeping in with the railway, but they had not been given the benefit of their own reserves in compensation. They had finally risen in revolt in 1885 in south Saskatchewan but had been swiftly defeated, largely because of the newly built railway that had enabled the militia from the east to be transported swiftly across Canada in the dead of winter.

Barry is proud of his heritage and at the same time has a fine sense of humour and a hedonistic approach to life. It was going to be fun climbing with him. Since I only had the one day we chose a straightforward local climb on Chinaman's Peak, a limestone mass just above Canmore. Its name is variously attributed to one of the Chinese railway workers who made the first ascent, or more dramatically to one who committed suicide by hurling himself down its precipitous north face.

We were going to climb its north-east ridge. After a fortnight of rail travel it was a delight to walk up through woods and over scree to the foot of the climb, although I couldn't help worrying about how fit I was going to be. Barry gallantly offered me the lead of the first pitch, largely because it was so easy, then led the next one up a steepening ramp to the foot of the serious climbing. At this stage it started to rain and Barry, the good guide, produced a bivouac tent for us to shelter in. It was a couple of hours before it stopped. With my limited time, and about eight pitches to go, we discussed whether we should turn back. Barry said it was my choice, and at this stage I just wanted to climb; I had no doubts.

'Let's go for it,' I said.

'We're going to be tight on time, you know,' replied Barry. 'How about me taking over as the guide?'

I exploded. It was a gut reaction, partly caused by the number of occasions recently when people have assumed that because of my age I no longer climb, or no longer do so seriously. There was some injured ego, but also I love climbing, and to be climbing means being out in front, picking out a line, playing the risk game, pushing the limits and revelling in the drop below your

ABOVE Barry Blanchard, world-class mountaineer, against the solid limestone
mass of Chinaman's Peak which he and Chris Bonington climbed

OPPOSITE Coachloads of tourists and ugly modern buildings disfigure some parts of the
Rockies, but it is still possible to find wild, unvisited regions

feet because if you do make a mistake you are going to fall. Barry meant well,
but that didn't limit my gut reaction.

'Like hell you will!' I fumed. 'This is my pitch and I'll lead it. I've never
been guided up a climb and I don't intend to start now. We're sharing the lead
and that's how we'll do it.'

I grabbed some gear, started up the pitch still furious, and climbed it as
fast as I could. It wasn't particularly difficult – white limestone with little
bulges and pockets in the rocks that fingers curled into, even the occasional
piton that had been hammered into cracks to clip into for protection. I ran out
the full length of rope, and by the time I had found a belay and brought Barry
up I was ashamed of my outburst.

We both spoke, almost at once.

'I'm afraid I went a bit over the top,' I said.

'Didn't mean to hurt your feelings – didn't realize you could climb so fast – you fair raced up that pitch,' he replied.

After that we settled into a fast easy rhythm of climbing, wasting no time, barely talking as we passed each other on stances, but enjoying each other's company and the quality of the climb. The final rope lengths led into a huge open corner that soared towards the top. It looked hard but the holds appeared by magic. By late afternoon we were on the summit, where we sat and talked about mutual friends, climbs and places. I wanted to climb with Barry again. Although he was nearly thirty years my junior and a much more powerful climber, we had found an equal footing and understanding.

I returned to my journey refreshed. I now had to travel to Jasper to rejoin the Canadian, the aluminium lozenge in which I had travelled from Toronto to Saskatoon and which had bypassed Calgary, going straight to Edmonton to the north and then on to Jasper. This meant driving along the tourist trail through Banff National Park. The scenery was magnificent with snow peaks and glaciers, ultramarine lakes and deep-cut gorges, but it had all been sanitized for the car- or coach-borne tourist with way-marked concrete paths leading to each signed and annotated viewpoint. Attained so easily and shared with so many, it became little more than a picture postcard in a gift shop. Halfway to Jasper the road passes a point where the broad, icy tongue of the Athabasca Glacier snakes towards some sprawling car parks and buildings built to cater for the crowds that come for the 'glacier experience'. A ride across it on a giant caterpillar tractor costs $18.50. My reaction was one of resentment at the crowds, the coaches and the ugliness of the buildings, and yet it did at least allow people to see a glacier perhaps for the first and only time in their lives. The Rockies are so vast that you only have to walk a few miles from the road and you can forget that it ever existed; go over a ridge on the skyline and it can be as wild and empty as when the first railway pioneers came searching for a way through the mountains.

At Jasper we had a day to wait for the tourist train and watched the mile-long freight trains, hauled by five locomotives at a time, slowly roll past the town on their long climb to Yellowhead Pass. Jasper itself is a tourist honeypot, full of motels, trinket shops and cafés, but it is crowded in by forest-clad hills and fine snow peaks are visible in the distance. The train was five hours late due to hurricane-force storms in Ontario over 100 miles away, but it didn't really seem to matter. There were gains and losses. Because we set out in the early evening we'd miss the view of Mount Robson, one of the giants of the Rockies, but we would see the Fraser River Gorge in the early morning instead of travelling through it by night. This was the final great challenge in the original building of the Canadian Pacific Railway.

Although this was my last night in a sleeper on the Canadian, I got up at 5 a.m. to see Ashcroft, reputed to be the driest place in Canada with only 18 centimetres of rain a year. It looked it, its arid hills of dirt and gravel sprinkled with cactus and sage, washed grey in the pre-dawn light, the Thompson River swirling in its deep-cut slot below. I was reminded of the Braldu Gorge in the Karakoram, which has only recently been penetrated by a precarious road clinging to its sides. Here there was not just one, but two railways, hugging either bank of the river, at times crossing each other from one side to the other in a complex piece of steel knitting, a symbol of the intense competition that existed between what became the state-owned Canadian National Railway and the original Canadian Pacific Railway. The latter was first in place, built largely by Chinese labour in 1885. It was a prodigious feat of engineering, up the Fraser Gorge and then on up the Thompson, through unstable shale cliffs, across tributaries of the river on wooden trestle bridges and tunnelling through spurs that jutted into the river. Many lives were lost, but the railway was pushed through to join up with the line coming in from the east on 7 November 1885 at Craigellachie, some 80 miles west of Rogers Pass, the high point of the route across the Selkirk Range. Donald Smith, who with George Stephen had been the driving force in the struggle to finance the railway, drove in the last spike to complete the line from Toronto to Vancouver and link the Atlantic with the Pacific; it had been achieved in just fifty-four months, almost six years ahead of its original schedule.

In our own tourist train, all that remained of the passenger link, we had reached the Fraser Canyon, passing places with evocative names like

OVERLEAF **The slim silver Canadian, on which Chris Bonington completed most of his journey across Canada**

Avalanche Alley, Jaws of Death Gorge and Suicide Rapids. Even today there is an element of risk from the frequent rockfalls that can sweep the tracks. We pulled into a siding to allow a freight train to pass. These are the bread and butter of the railway network and can still compete effectively with road transportation, each train hauling the equivalent of three hundred 40-tonne truckloads of merchandise that would crowd and pollute the roads.

As the sun rose the valley widened, enabling the river to meander gently through lush farmland. Rafts of lumber floated down, leaving escaped treetrunks marooned against the banks like gigantic matchsticks. Towns became more frequent and more expansive, slowly merging into the urban sprawl of Vancouver. The journey was nearly over. I had taken almost three weeks to make it, although I could have completed it in five days had I travelled continuously. In that period I had visited more widely separated places than most members of the population of Canada have done, and I had had a broad, if admittedly superficial, overview of this huge, sprawling country.

I had a feeling of real affection for it in the new friends I had made and the old ones I had caught up with. I had started with preconceptions that Canadians and their history were rather dull, and that they had an identity problem – not sure if they were Americans, expatriates or what. I think I was wrong on practically all counts. I sensed a feeling of quiet satisfaction in being Canadian that was agreeably free of nationalism or jingoism; a feeling that this is a great place to live came across from so many different people. There was also a sense of being laid back, less of that eager-beaver dynamism that I've noticed south of the Canadian border, a greater capacity to enjoy leisure and a feeling of care for this huge land. I know these are generalizations. There is crime, violence, poverty and greed in this country as there is in every other country in the world, but I think there is perhaps less than in some other places I have visited. Even the great debate about Canadian French independence seemed less acute when I talked to people on the way; they were telling me that it was the creation of the politicians, that when it comes to the crunch the French Canadians will want to stay part of Canada. I hope they do. And I had eaten well all the way across Canada, on the train, in hotels and in diners – stacks of well-prepared food delivered in a wonderfully friendly way, whether in the Royal York Hotel or in a little guest house in Moosonee. I'd enjoyed the informality of the people, so that I could feel at home in tee-shirts, shorts and sandals wherever I went, in the cities as well as in the countryside.

By now downtown Vancouver was beginning to dominate the skyline, not as compact and domineering as Toronto or Montreal but more scattered and seemingly relaxed, as I suspected and hoped Canada's major western city would be. I was sitting in the rear car of the train. The assistant conductor, a tall impressive man, had the rear door open and a walkie-talkie clutched in his hand. We had been in a wide loop through a kind of railway graveyard of deserted freight yards, so that the train could be backed into Vancouver Station to enable the first-class passengers to have the minimum distance to walk to the terminal.

In the midst of this desolation we reached a set of points. The conductor spoke into the handset and the train drew to a halt. He leaped out, walked over to the lever, heaved it to change the points and returned to the train. It was as if we were in the middle of the wilderness, or perhaps on a little side line in Ireland, rather than just outside a huge Canadian city in the flagship train of VIA. Another command and we were on the move again, backing our way down the line towards the station platform.

He murmured into the handset, 'Three more, VIA 1,' to have it each time repeated by the engineer.

'Two car.'

'One car.'

'Half a car, VIA.'

'Thirty feet.'

'Twenty feet.'

'Ten feet.'

'That'll do and you stop, VIA 1,' and the train drew smoothly to a halt, a centimetre from the buffers.

He turned to me, deadpan, not a trace of a smile. 'That was as good as a lunar landing.'

'Neil Armstrong couldn't have done it better,' I replied.

Argentina: the Andes to Patagonia

BUCK HENRY

IT STARTS HERE, this journey, at the top, high up in the Andes. Over there, to the west, across those impressive ice-capped peaks – the most formidable frontier between two countries in the Western Hemisphere – is Chile. Bolivia is to the north. Over there, to the east, is Paraguay. Not unlike the citizens of a number of other countries – well, maybe all other countries – most Argentines have something unflattering to say about their neighbours. The Bolivians are dopes; the folks in Paraguay are thugs; the Chileans are bandits.

I had an idea for a story I wanted to write. A screenplay. I wanted it to be about a man, an American, who tries to leave his life behind, find a new identity, disappear. I talked to some people about it. There was a consensus. Argentina. That's the place. Filled with immigrants who disappeared from their home countries, from their families, from their histories. Cultures that disappeared. People who disappeared by choice; people who disappeared by decree.

I'm on the Tren a las Nubes – the Train to the Clouds – which carries tourists from the city of Salta, the capital of the northernmost province, to this place 3600 metres up in the cold thin air of the Puna, the word for these

Buck Henry on the platform at Ingeniero Maury, named after the American engineer who built this extraordinary railway line among the high peaks of the Andes desolate wind-blown lands near the top of the Andes. Every day in the spring and summer months this train makes its journey to the top. It stops just long enough for the tourists, many of them exhausted from the ten-hour ride, some of them panting or clutching their altitude-induced headaches, to get out and take some photographs of the scenery or of the Indians – the adults who are selling home-woven sweaters, pullovers and caps of alpaca and vicuña, and the children who hope to make a couple of pesos by posing with their bedraggled animals – goats, lambs, a bored and resentful-looking llama.

It's a spring day and the sun is warm, but the sudden winds that come barrelling down the mountainsides are strong enough to knock you off your feet and cold enough to freeze your eyeballs. The view of the peaks is not nearly as spectacular as it was from miles away. We're too close. It's a little too forbidding. And it's hard to imagine that these people – the Coya Indians, probably descendants of a pocket of Incas who were stranded in this place perhaps a hundred years ago – actually live and work here, mostly in the mines. Farther up the line there's a border crossing, a mining town from which, every day, a big red and yellow diesel locomotive pulls a train of grey, steel, ore-carrying dump cars down the line to Salta. Once a week they hitch up a passenger coach – a leftover from some 1940s train, with worn leather seats and ceiling fans that don't work. No tourists on this one. No one, in fact, of European descent. Only copper-skinned brown-eyed Coya, carrying their goods to the big city market. There's no dining car; the Indians couldn't afford it if there were one. By the time the train gets to Salta, a trip of at least thirty-six hours, the carriage and its patient occupants are covered with a fine brown dust blown in by the Puna wind.

On the way up, I got off the tourist train and hitched a ride on the other. The dump cars were empty. There was no one aboard other than the chief engineer, an assistant, a conductor and a young man in the last car – a kind of living quarters for the workers. It had a tiny curtained-off area with a bed, a few books and some centrefold girls tacked to the wall. In the middle of the car were a couple of broken wooden benches and a chair, drawn up close to a wood-burning stove which the man kept feeding from a metal wood-bin.

Most of the time I spent sitting in the doorway, looking out at the extraordinary moonscape, the quality and density of the light changing as the sun disappeared and reappeared from behind the Andean peaks, the lower cliffs changing in colour according to their metallic content – brown, grey and green. There's a stretch of one or two hours through land that reminds me of the Arizona desert; giant cacti stand, individually, aloof from each other, like strange impassive observers, some of them with a small red flower or two sprouting from their green hides, giving them a jaunty if other-worldly look.

The assistant and the conductor come back and join us, and the young man whose job I can't really figure out makes a cup of maté for us. It's the national beverage, although I've never seen it served in a hotel or on a restaurant menu. A kettle of water boils on the stove. The young man has a cup – more like a half gourd – on top of which he places a strainer. From a box of powdered green maté leaves he packs the strainer, tamping it down like tobacco in a pipe, then pours the water over it. There's a metal straw that sticks through a hole in the strainer. He passes the cup to me and I draw in a mouthful which, of course, burns my tongue, eliciting a grimace from me and a polite laugh from my companions. The cup is passed from man to man and around again until the tea is gone. The taste – not unlike boiled marijuana – is definitely an acquired one. And the residue keeps getting into my mouth. It takes practice.

But on the tourist train – the Tren a las Nubes – there's a club car where ham and cheese sandwiches, coffee and candy bars are sold. And two-peso cellophane packets of coca leaves which are made into tea or, according to instructions, are wadded up, twenty or so leaves at a time, placed in the cheek and allowed to dissolve. Its mild narcotic effect is supposed to suppress the appetite and alleviate altitude sickness. The taste is nothing to write home about, but it's better than the shortness of breath and pounding headaches that attack enough passengers for the medical car always to be full of people who stagger in to lie down in one of the two bunk beds, get their blood pressure taken or gasp into oxygen masks. There are, in fact, oxygen tanks and masks at the end of every car and a couple of female attendants to minister to the afflicted. The tidy bathrooms are solid tin or zinc modules, although the toilets themselves are open holes to the trackbed below. Posters affixed to the wall warn of cholera.

This line is one of the great triumphs of railway construction. Built by an engineer from Philadelphia named Ricardo Fontaine Maury, it took from

ABOVE Refreshments on the Train to the Clouds

OPPOSITE This freight train carries ore down to Salta from
a little Andean mining town inhabited by Coya Indians.
Passengers can ride the train once a week – their journey takes
thirty-six hours and they arrive covered in dust

1921 to 1948 to complete. It crosses rivers, moves through tunnels and across bridges and viaducts so steep that clouds move below their steel bases and we seem to be hanging in the air. There are double and triple zigzags in which the train has to be backed up and then forward again in order to gain altitude. And in one place the train makes a huge circle and passes under its own track.

As though to emphasize the difficulty of this feat of engineering, we pass a lonely graveyard on a hill in which lie the remains of workers – foreigners mostly – who died from accidents while building the line. Among those who worked here and survived was Josip Broz, known later as Marshal Tito, dictator of Yugoslavia.

Along the way we pass ugly mining towns or tiny communities where small groups of Indians live in the abandoned shacks of railway workers. Not much moves – a few cattle, goats, some skinny horses, a wild hare making a mad dash across the tracks and the inevitable dogs of no known breed.

The train makes a short stop at the small town of Ingeniero Maury, named after the man from Philadelphia. He's buried here. I get off to see if I can find his grave. There's no one around except a few Indian kids who run away when I approach them. It's very quiet. Even the wind has stopped. Off to one side of the tracks there's a football field. On the other side there's a house, and in its back yard a little stone and earth igloo-shaped structure, a kind of family shrine, filled with offerings to the Pacha Mama, the Latin American mother earth figure.

About an hour away from Ingeniero Maury, near a town called Santa Rosa de Tastil, are the remains of a lost city. Here, over a half dozen hills, is spread the pattern of a place where, perhaps, thousands lived and worked about a millennium ago. Low stone walls and the remains of streets are all that are left now. Fragments of animal bones and pottery crunch underfoot. Archaeologists have found the burial site of a chieftain. With him are the bones of a woman, two children and a dog. Even today the practice continues: when a Coya man dies, his dog is sacrificed and buried with him.

Around 1400 the city was abandoned. No one knows why. The inhabitants simply disappeared.

It's beginning to get dark as the train makes its way toward the outskirts of Salta. Most of the travellers are asleep, in spite of the efforts of some entertainers who wander through the cars, singing and strumming guitars. One pair, however, gets their attention: a middle-aged man in a gaudy sports jacket who plays guitar accompaniment to the songs of a teenage boy who looks like a young Michael Jackson when he still resembled an Earthling, and who sings traditional tangos in a beautiful high clear voice.

As the lights of the outlying districts appear, the passengers are asked to lower the metallic screens that are placed behind every window as a defence against the rocks that the shanty-town occupants like to throw at the train.

Salta is bigger than I expected. The main square is a reminder of what the old colonial city must have looked like. But most of the surrounding streets are a garish jumble of neon-lit shops, fast-food joints and run-down houses.

This is the day of Salta's most important yearly religious celebration – the procession of the 'Virgen' and the Cristo del Milagro – which explains why the city is so crowded and why, on the train trip down from the Andes, I had seen little groups of pilgrims making their way south on foot, whole families, sometimes carrying a cross or banner of some kind. Many of them have arrived over the past few days. There were Indians, Mestizos (the descendants of Euro-Indians), the poor and the very poor, sleeping in the streets, sometimes in front of the more fashionable shops whose windows display goods from Italy and Britain and America – electronic equipment, clothing and shoes, a pair of which costs more than many of these families make in a year.

By noon the main square and the streets around it are packed with people waiting for the big event. The bells in the cathedral towers start to ring. I can see a dozen or so men in the towers struggling with the ropes. There are bells of different sizes and the pattern of music they're playing is intricate, if not melodious. And deafening. Even from hundreds of yards away, conversation is virtually impossible. One can see that the ears of many of the priests, nuns and dignitaries on the cathedral steps are stuffed with cotton wool.

The bells stop and a loudspeakered female voice whose owner I cannot see sings several unfamiliar hymns in an equally unfamiliar key. Then a brass band plays and the statues begin to emerge from the cathedral, each one borne on a huge litter, carried on the backs of a dozen straining, sweating men who

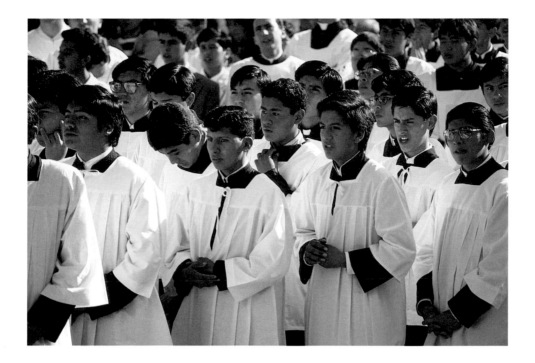

OPPOSITE Religious figures are carried in procession through
the town during Salta's religious festival

ABOVE During the noisy and colourful ceremony anthems are
sung to the statues of Christ and the Virgin Mary

have to struggle mightily to get them down the steps and on to a float. The first statue is of the Weeping Virgin and, as it is moved down the street behind cordons of military officers and police, the huge crowd responds, waving white handkerchiefs, shouting approval, many crying.

Then the two principal statues, of Mary and Jesus, emerge and the crowd erupts again. They too are carried off in a procession that moves around the city, surrounded by important church and civic officials and soldiers in their dress uniforms, followed by thousands of citizens and visitors. The statues themselves are tall and imposing; their heads are so high that they can almost be touched by the people who are leaning out of their second- and third-storey windows.

There are slightly different versions of the legend behind this event but the narrative goes something like this. In 1592 the statue of Jesus was given to the people of Salta by Spain. A hundred years later a massive earthquake hit the city and almost destroyed it.

Subsequently, a priest had a vision in which he was given a message which he dutifully passed on to the people of Salta: if the citizens mended their ways and went regularly to church, and if each year on the anniversary of the big quake the church officials displayed the two statues, the city would be spared from further devastation. So far, it appears to have worked. There have been many earthquakes but they have been far less dramatic.

The procession moves to the north end of town where the crowds, now grown to tens of thousands, surround a platform from which the archbishop makes a very long speech which is followed by a couple of religious anthems sung to the two statues. Standing with the archbishop are twenty or so of the region's most important political figures, including Salta's Governor and Senator and their wives, who are smiling dutifully although their feet in their expensive high-heeled shoes must be killing them. The Senator is running for the Governor's office in the upcoming election and, since he and the Governor are of opposing political parties, the two families are carefully not acknowledging each other.

Back at the railway station, I find out that the train to Buenos Aires has been rescheduled. As I am to discover over the next few weeks, this is not an

132

uncommon occurrence. I am told that I can take a bus ride – a long bus ride – to the town of Tucumán where I should – might – possibly get a train to B.A. And to my surprise I find when I get to the bus station that there is, indeed, a bus about to leave and that it is a state-of-the-art, roomy, air-conditioned, Brazilian-made superbus complete with extremely attractive uniformed stewardesses.

Since I was last here, a few years ago, the Argentines have grown richer and poorer. The government's determined efforts at privatizing the economy have made many new millionaires and put hundreds of thousands out of work. In Buenos Aires there are huge new glittering shopping malls and scores of new restaurants where the oligarchy, the new rich and their ostentatiously dressed children can dine. But the endless row of great steak houses just outside the city proper where, ten years ago, the best steak dinners in the world cost the equivalent of six or seven dollars and where entire families of meat-loving Argentinians gorged until one or two in the morning, now stand half empty.

The new rate of exchange for Argentine currency has one thing going for it. It's easy to compute. The peso is pegged at par with the dollar. One peso equals one dollar. That's about all it has in its favour. People with access to dollars have got very, very rich. Everyone else is in deep trouble. So, although the crushing inflation rate of a few years ago has been brought under control, millions of those who were once safely in the middle class have found their standard of living virtually disappearing. Savings are being wiped out as they struggle to keep up in an economy that's tightening its belt and squeezing the life out of them.

On the train ride from Tucumán to Buenos Aires I sit opposite a man peering at a tattered Spanish–English dictionary. He looks a little tattered himself. And no wonder. He's a secondary school English teacher named Jorge, and he hasn't been paid in two months because the federal government has stripped its budget of money for education and thrown the problem back to the provinces. And the provinces – most of them – are broke. Jorge's salary has been frozen, while the cost of living has gone up 50 or 60 per cent.

Jorge calls himself a taxi-teacher, and explains that the term 'taxi' refers to those members of the professional class who have to hold two, three and four different jobs to survive – although it's unlikely that men and women in his position are actually able to afford taxis to carry them from one job to another.

'When do you sleep?' I ask him.

He smiles a small, grim smile. 'I would be sleeping now, if I were not talking to you.'

In a televised presidential speech yesterday – and not a day goes by, it seems, when there is not a televised presidential speech – President Menem discussed the pain of privatization and likened it to 'surgery without anaesthetic'.

'What happens,' I ask Jorge, 'when you and thousands like you simply have to quit teaching?'

Another grim smile. 'That's the idea,' he says. 'Half the teachers will quit and then the school system has the excuse to enrol half the number of students.'

This vicious circle seems to be the pattern for workers everywhere, and it's particularly dramatic where the railway system is concerned. Menem has talked about – boasted about, actually – having reduced the working staff of the railroads from a bloated, useless two hundred thousand to a practical fifteen thousand, and selling off the lines to private investors. So fewer people with fewer jobs are now travelling from the outlying districts into the cities. Fewer fares are being paid. Trains are reducing the number of people they carry; more trains are being taken off the line. And railway workers are watching their jobs disappear.

I was hoping to discuss this with Tucumán's provincial governor who, rumour had it, was going to be riding on the train. He seems to be a man with a colourful past, having gone from being a shoeshine boy to a pop star and then rising (or falling, depending on your point of view) to the position of Governor. I'd hoped to find out if he knew of America's guitar-wielding Governor of bygone years, Singin' Jim Folsom, or if he was familiar with the present-day Republican member of Congress, Sonny Bono, late of 'Sonny and Cher'. But the Governor apparently changed his plans and thus avoided what would have been undoubtedly a stirring cross-cultural dialogue.

The train pulls into Buenos Aires' Retiro Station, now worn and shabby with grass growing between the tracks, birds flying around inside and a number

Buenos Aires' shops are as smart as those of Bond Street or Fifth Avenue

of lame, homeless dogs wandering around. There is a major incongruity that greets the eye here: many of the station's walls are decorated with wildly impressionistic murals – paintings of trains, naked women, dogs, planes and machines.

The few people standing around, waiting for trains that may or may not be still scheduled, seem to be paying no attention to the sight of these strange creations. When I ask some of the hopeful passengers if they can tell me who's responsible for the art they just shake their heads, sometimes with a little embarrassed giggle that seems to mean 'Don't blame me – I'm just standing here.' Finally, a station official in what passes for a uniform tells me that the murals are the work of a painter who lives a couple of hundred yards away in a building on the grounds of the station that, for some reason that he, the official, obviously can't fathom, has been given to the artist by the government to live and work in. The official touches his finger to his head and gives me a sideways look that suggests we are talking about someone who is either eccentric or dangerous or both.

I have twenty-four hours or more before I may or may not get the next train I'm looking for, so I go in search of the mysterious muralist. He's not hard to find. The abandoned warehouse that he's taken over is surrounded by his *oeuvre*: brightly coloured sculptures ingeniously composed of giant hunks of abandoned railway equipment: wheels, pistons, oil cans, nuts, bolts, funnels and so on. And his name, Regazzoni, is scrawled on the walls of his home along with various dire warnings to trespassers.

As I approach the door I can hear opera playing – blasting, rather – at ear-shattering volume, mixed with loud laughter and the odd female scream. I knock on the side of the door, which is actually a beaded curtain, I yell his name, and a few moments later I am deluged with several dozen squeezed-out tubes of paint thrown through the door, followed by the thrower, Regazzoni himself, large, round, wearing traditional paint-smeared pants and shirt and sporting a mass of curly black hair held in place by a pair of welder's goggles.

The shower of paint tubes, I learn later, is actually a friendlier greeting than the one that strangers are usually confronted with – a bellowed warning in Spanish: *'I don't have any money.'*

Over the next few hours I learn the following: his name is Carlos Alberto Regazzoni. He is known to one and all as Rega. Once a kerosene salesman of no distinction, he was at some point inspired or traumatized (depending on whom he's telling to the story to) by a train or the sight of a train or the sound of a train or maybe just the idea of a train. That was many years ago. Since that murky event he has been obsessed by trains, painting them and creating sculptures of them, becoming in the process the artist laureate of traindom.

The gigantic warehouse he lives in – he calls it his factory – is filled with his paintings, hundreds, maybe thousands of them, oversized, violent with colour, representing all kinds of trains, passing behind, in front of and between large naked women and slinking curs. They hang on every inch of wall space. They're stacked on the floor. They're on racks. Large wooden tables are groaning under the weight of hundreds of his painted plates. His sculptures fill up any extra space and there are small curtained areas for a tiny bedroom, a primitive bathroom and a wall of stereo equipment with CDs of operas scattered around. Pieces of old trains have been converted to domestic use; a massive engine boiler has been transmogrified into a fireplace.

There are women all over the place, lounging on chairs and couches, fiddling at the stove, dancing around. Rega has nicknames for each of them but, in general, refers to them as his *chicas* (his girls) or, sometimes, his little cats. They may or may not be his models. There is a strong suggestion that theirs is an occupation that causes them to spend a lot of time on dark streets. They seem to like him a lot, and the more he insults them the louder they laugh.

In case I should be under the misapprehension that all his work ends up in his home, he shows me photos of his paintings that are hanging in houses and museums all over the world and of other murals in other railway stations, particularly in Paris where the French government has given him large spaces in the Gare du Nord and the Gare de l'Est to display his work.

'They love my work in France,' he bellows. 'And in Germany they love me. And I am loved in England. But here in Argentina they are too stupid to appreciate me, and besides they are afraid of me because I am dangerous.' He says: 'Da-a-a-nger-r-r-ous.' This last point he illustrates by pulling up his shirt and proudly displaying a scar about a foot and a half long which, he explains, was given to him by a man who placed his hand on one of Rega's girlfriend's buttocks and, in the resulting dispute, used his knife on Rega who, in turn, attacked the man with a broken bottle and killed him. Or, maybe, it was Rega's hand on the man's girlfriend's buttocks or, possibly, it was the girlfriend of someone who knifed Rega and – well, it's complicated.

All this, in a mixture of Spanish, broken English and fractured French, while emphasizing his points with a massive carving knife that he's using like a machete against a side of beef, the size of half a rowing-boat, curved and held together by a mass of yard-long ribs, that he'd been cooking over an open fire in the back of the factory when I arrived and that he's now hacking up for our dinner. The guests are a brace of *chicas*, some of Rega's assistants and a selection of unidentified hangers-on. The dinner itself consists entirely of xylophones of beef, loaves of bread and champagne.

Whenever someone new appears, usually another woman on a temporary break from whatever street she's working, there's a lot of kissing. Argentines like to kiss. They kiss on first acquaintance. They kiss hello. They

OVERLEAF **The grandiose presidential palace in Buenos Aires**

kiss goodbye. They kiss for thank you. It's exhausting. My new Argentine friends who, after a few hours of champagne and beef, I am beginning to feel are my closest comrades, nevertheless seem to be unable to grasp my name. 'Bob' is about as close as they can get. So I settle for it.

Whenever anyone yawns, looks tired or threatens to leave, Rega stands and waves the carving knife around. The evening turns into night and the night turns into morning and, finally, after an endless round of goodbye kisses and a promise to return in a week or two for a *real* party with twice as many *chicas* and the other half of the cow, I am permitted to make an exhausted exit.

There's a café in Buenos Aires' fashionable Recoleta district where, ostensibly, politicians and journalists hang out. I have an appointment there with a writer named Sylvina Walger.

Before meeting her I take a few minutes to visit the nearby Recoleta Cemetery where, amid the ostentatious monuments and crypts, lie the bones of many of Argentina's famous and infamous. Among them are Eva Perón, whose relatively unpretentious mausoleum is still a daily magnet for black-garbed, teary-eyed women who come to place fresh flowers and pray for her return; and the great Argentine heavyweight prizefighter, Luis 'Angel' Firpo, known as the Wild Bull of the Pampas, who in 1923 unleashed a mighty right that knocked the champion, Jack Dempsey, out of the ring.

At the café, where a number of notably older gentlemen are entertaining a number of notably younger women, I meet Sylvina. The book she's just written, *Pizza with Champagne*, has made her no friends at all in the upper circles of society and government, focusing, as it does, on fiscal corruption, nepotism and the personal peccadillos of the rich and famous.

What was once a city-wide appetite for psychoanalysis among the *Porteños*, which is what the residents of Buenos Aires call themselves (there's a section of Buenos Aires where the percentage of resident analysts is so high that the area is known as 'Villa Freud'), has been replaced by a passion for plastic surgery. I've heard stories of practitioners of the fine art of de-ageing who have made over their wives to look like their mistresses (probably not vice versa); of a doctor who operates on himself every five years or so; and of another who specializes in giving women the 'Evita look'.

Sylvina Walger, an attractive, animated blonde who seems to take great delight in her funny nasty anecdotes, claims that President Menem himself has been operated on so many times that his official portraits have to be doctored every year so that people will recognize him. Menem's wife – the Menems are separated and their various family scandals are an endless soap opera for the daily newspapers – thanks to the surgeon's knife, now looks younger than her own daughter, asserts Sylvina. She adds that Señora Menem has so much gold thread in her face that if she opens her mouth too wide her eyes pop out. It's a compelling image.

I ask Sylvina if she's ever nervous about writing things that a very few years ago could have cost her her freedom, possibly even her life. She smiles and then looks around – just for a moment – as though to see who might be listening. Then she gestures to the bag in her lap: 'My passport is in order and I have a paid ticket to another country.'

I go to Constitución Station to find out about the train I'm hoping to get on this evening: the Buenos Aires–Bariloche train. The man in the information booth points to the schedule board. It is blank. The train that has been rescheduled for this evening has been rescheduled. In the last twenty-four hours, the entire departure schedule has been rewritten. I ask why. It's a stupid question. Nobody knows. There are knots of people standing around staring at the empty schedule board with vaguely puzzled looks. There are five large station clocks on the walls above. They all show a different time. The information man asks me if I want to put my name on a list for reservations on whatever train might be leaving at some future unknown hour. I write 'Franz Kafka' and move on.

Since I can't go to Patagonia, I'll go west – to the vast, flat plains of the Pampas. It takes a long time to get out of this huge, sprawling city. One third of the entire population of Argentina lives in the capital and its surrounding districts. As far as the *Porteños* are concerned, the rest of their country barely exists. Most of the city folks, the educated ones, the privileged, are far more interested in what happens in Europe than in the affairs of the unsophisticated northern provinces, or in the world of the gaucho to the west, or in the lives of those who are eccentric enough to dwell in the remote stretches of Patagonia.

The train passes through a number of small towns, most of which are named after political and military heroes. And suddenly we are in the rich land of the Pampas – endless virtually treeless vistas where the great herds of cattle and sheep graze and where the country's main crops are grown.

In the town of Coronel Suárez I am met by Horacio Araya, the tall, handsome owner of a ranch – an *estancia* – a fifteen-minute drive in his pick-up truck from the station. Horacio and his wife, Maria Estela, their daughter and their four sons live in town, but often spend their weekends on the ranch.

Coronel Suárez isn't very impressive. There are some nice homes where the *estancia* owners live, and a lot of stores selling farm equipment and dry goods. There's a fairly large German community here. Some time in the 1800s they left Germany for a better life in Russia, didn't think much of it and made the long crossing to Argentina. They don't speak German any longer. Hardly anyone in this country speaks their grandparents' native tongue any longer. Strangely, most Argentines speak Spanish with what sounds like a slight Italian accent.

Bumping along over the dusty country roads of the Pampas, it's hard not to think of the history of the Americas of the last couple of hundred years. Thousands of refugees from other countries, from cities in the east, coming to find a new life, a new kind of freedom.

The Pampas, like America's Wild West, fought its bloody battles. The Indians against the new settlers. The Army against the Indians. The Indians were, of course, exterminated but it took a determined army to do it. For years the railways had to be protected by a system of scouts on horseback and pilot locomotives that ran in front of the trains in case logs were placed across the tracks. There are even stories of packs of Indians attacking trains by trying to lasso the locomotive stacks.

Horacio's gauchos wear jeans and sweaters and boots or sneakers, and most of them wear berets. It is, as it has always been, a hard and dangerous life. I've been reading – or trying to read – the epic novel of gaucho life, *Don Segundo*

The subject of this statue at the Retiro Station is less well known outside
Argentina than the ship named after him, which was sunk in the
Falklands War – the *Belgrano*

142

Sombra, a highly romanticized view of life on the plains, of cattle drives, knife fights, boozing and whoremongering; but it seems to be both patronizing and sentimental.

The Arayas' *estancia* home is simple and beautiful, modelled on a South African native house, with a white-walled circular living room whose high-domed ceiling is supported by gum tree logs. Off to one side of the house is the family's practice polo field. Polo is, of course, the passion of the landed gentry here. Three of Horacio's sons have left their university educations behind and are travelling around the world playing polo matches. Horacio himself has played for many of Argentina's championship teams. The teams travel with their own horses, the highly trained polo ponies that are bred especially for the game. And there have to be fresh horses available for every chukka. A chukka lasts about four minutes. It's a very expensive obsession.

All the members of the family ride as easily as they walk. Even the grandchildren, some of them as young as three, have their own ponies which they command with enviable expertise.

Although it's the beginning of spring, there's a bitter cold wind blowing across the Pampas. The wind hardly ever stops here, and is strong enough to have caused the thick wooden beams of the polo field's goalposts to bend at a thirty-degree angle. It's been a year without rain, and many of the crops have failed to mature. Windmills that pump underground water to the surface dot the landscape, but their arms are tied down because the wind is too strong for them to operate safely.

Several stands of poplar trees, planted near the house, act with surprising efficiency as protection from the wind. We have lunch outside. A couple of sides of sheep, skinned and skewered, lean against an open fire. While the family and I sit at a long wooden table a dozen gauchos sit on the ground nearby, slicing up the joints of lamb with their ever-present razor-sharp *facones*.

A gaucho from another *estancia* has been invited to bring his guitar. Seated on a chair in a semi-circle of his gaucho comrades, he sings us a series of cowboy laments which, judging from the audience's response, seem to be equally funny and sad – songs about women and horses, the former being the cause of much more trouble than the latter, not to mention far less necessary in the general scheme of things.

Maria Estela explains to me that in the gaucho cosmos it is not only more difficult to understand the horse than the woman, but it is infinitely more important. She tries to translate for me one long ballad about a gaucho whose wife is so ill that, in order to buy medicine for her, he has to sell his horse, his boots, and finally, his knife. It's a real heart-breaker.

After lunch I ride on a round-up with the boss. The gauchos use a saddle with a top layer of thick sheepskin that make it the most comfortable saddle on which I've ever ridden. But the stirrups are strange – wooden slats in which a narrow incision is made to stick the toes in. The horse is fast and easy to handle, although he seems to spend a lot of time looking back at me as though trying to figure out what this foreigner is doing on his back.

Beef is the staple of the Argentinian diet. It's cheap and plentiful, and the grass-fed cattle are turned into the tastiest steaks in the world. *Lomo*, it's called. Every decent restaurant serves it: *lomo* fried, *lomo* broiled, *lomo* barbecued, *lomo asado*; and every self-respecting Argentine eats it at least once a day. Horacio tells me that a new scientific study has proved that the Argentinians' endless consumption of beef has had no measurable effect on their cholesterol level. Who am I to argue? I ask Horacio what happens to a vegetarian. He says: 'We give him a ticket and send him abroad.'

The loud and plaintive voices of the two hundred or so cattle mix with the whoops of the whip- and lariat-swinging gauchos and the barking of the dogs which run skilfully and fearlessly in and out of the herd. By the time the round-up is over it's late afternoon. The sun, a huge red and orange ball, settles down slowly and, as it touches the earth, spreads a magenta line along the horizon like a giant broken egg yolk.

I've figured it out. If I can get back to Buenos Aires by tomorrow I can get a train to Behie Blanca. From there to Viedma, where I can get another train to Ingeniero Jacobacci and from there another train to Maiten where I can pick up the Patagonian Express. This will take a little bit of willpower and an enormous amount of sheer dumb luck. It's worth a try.

The next morning I am at the Coronel Suárez station early, just in time for the stationmaster to tell me that the train to B.A. has left only fifteen minutes ago but, if I can somehow get a ride, I can catch it at the next station.

Outside the station there's a man in a railway company repair truck. I explain my problem to him and ask his advice. He tells me to get in the truck. Then he drives on to the trackbed, gets out, uses a lever of some kind to lower a second set of tyreless metal wheels on to the tracks themselves, turns on the engine and off we go, whizzing down the tracks like something out of a Bugs Bunny cartoon.

A half-hour later he pulls up near the next station where my missed train has stopped, lets me out, jiggers the track wheels back up and drives off the tracks and on to the road and away.

A few hours later I'm back in Buenos Aires, where I find out that the train to Viedma will leave the next morning. I will have faith. I will also have an afternoon and an evening to spend here.

My first stop is the Plaza de Mayo, where for almost two decades there has taken place on every Thursday afternoon one of the saddest and most moving processions in any country's history. This Thursday is no different and by two o'clock they have begun to gather – the Mothers of the Disappeared.

In 1976 the generals took over the government in a bloodless military coup, throwing out of office and into exile Perón's widow and third wife, Isabelita, and her crackpot personal secretary, José López Reza, who had been conducting psychic rituals over Evita Perón's embalmed body in an effort to transfer her spiritual powers into Isabelita.

Exploiting the fear of a Communist insurgency, for the next nine years the military governed the country like a concentration camp. They ran the economy into the ground. They started the pointless bloody war for the Falkland Islands. And in their frenzy to assure ideological uniformity they conducted a more intense and evil conflict – the so-called 'dirty war' – on their own people, on those who didn't agree with their policies. And the families and friends and supporters of those who didn't agree. Upwards of thirty thousand citizens – men, women and children – disappeared.

That's when the mothers began to march – in a circle around a

**At the Recoleta Cemetery a young woman brings flowers
to the grave of Eva Perón, *née* Duarte**

monument in the square across from the building from where the generals ruled. First just a few very brave ones, and then scores and then hundreds.

There are not as many today as there were when I was here seven years ago. Some have died; some are too old, too infirm to walk. But those who have survived have been joined now by others – husbands, relatives, friends and younger people. There is an organization of the Children of the Disappeared and the Mothers and Grandmothers hope that these younger ones will carry on their symbolic procession as a memorial to justice eternally deferred.

There's a white circle painted on the concrete around the monument. The Mothers walk the circle. They wear white scarves, some with the names of their lost loved ones embroidered on them. Many have buttons on their coats with pictures of sons and daughters – childhood photos, school photos, wedding photos. All these smiling faces are now gone – kidnapped, tortured, killed, thrown from planes into the sea, mutilated, dismembered, scattered and buried in unknown places.

Menem has issued a general amnesty to the military and the secret police and the goons that worked for them. After all the hearings and all the commissions, only a few top military officials were tried and convicted and sent to live in relative comfort on a military base.

A woman walks by with five buttons pinned to her coat. It is embarrassing to look too closely at the photos, too rude an invasion of her personal agony, even though she stands there in front of you, staring at your face, asking you to look, to share, if not her grief, at least her rage.

Renée had three children – two sons and a daughter. They disappeared. When she talks about them you cannot help but feel that even now – almost two decades later – she keeps alive the infinitesimal hope that by some miracle one of them will be found alive. Or, perhaps, it is just something that a stranger – someone who has not lived through it and is not even able to imagine living through it – has the freedom to hope for.

I am embarrassed at asking her to talk about it, even though it's clear that she wants to, that she must. I am embarrassed that I can talk about it with her and not cry. I am embarrassed that I almost do cry; my relation to such emotion – to such events – is so second-hand.

Renée is quite old now. Her husband died some years ago. She will have no grandchildren to watch grow up. I think the reason she stays alive is to walk the white line.

There's a section of the city that no reasonable person would walk at night. Even during the day it's pretty creepy. The main market was here. It's now just a huge skeleton of a structure, surrounded by slum buildings on which hang broken and rusted signs for hotels that are long gone. One of the streets that runs off the old market is called Gardel Place. This is where Carlos Gardel, the great singer and composer of tangos, lived for a short time. He is a cultural god in Argentina and has streets, plazas and subway stations named after him all over Latin America. He recorded over a thousand songs before he died in 1935, still young, in a plane crash in Medellín, Colombia.

There's a faded, scarred painting of Gardel on one of the walls of Gardel Place. It shows him wearing his customary fedora and his huge toothy grin. Half boulevardier, half gangster, he looks like a cross between John Travolta and Fernandel.

A short way down this dismal street is a local store-front headquarters of the Peronista party. Juan Perón, too, is still a god in some parts of Argentina, particularly in the poorest sections where they remember the political power he gave to the dispossessed, the workers and the unions. Even though it's night, the lights are on and two elderly women are sitting in the dimly lit room, keeping watch over a small religious shrine at one end and hand-tinted portraits of Perón in a formal military uniform and Evita in a white ballgown that stare benignly down from the walls.

The tango keeps trying to die – like fado music in Portugal or ragtime in the States – but there are always enough people who won't let it go. Tango seems to embarrass the sophisticated and is irrelevant to the children of rock and roll, except for those few – and maybe more than a few who still respond to its raw sentiment and earnest themes of yearning – who long for lost love, lost homeland, lost innocence. These are the people who gather not in the kitschy over-priced tourist traps but in small run-down dance halls – private clubs – where they listen to the music and practise the intricate, sensuous rhythms of the dance.

One of these clubs is San Telmo. The members arrive around nine in the

While many of Britain's red telephone boxes have been replaced and turned into trendy shower cabinets, similar ones are still a familiar sight on the streets of Buenos Aires

evening, once a week: couples of all ages, elderly single men, dignified in suits and ties that look like they might have worn them at their weddings a hundred years ago, and young pretty girls in short black skirts and black leather high-heeled dancing boots that they bring in their handbags or backpacks to change into from their Keds and Reeboks.

There's not much conversation and, in spite of the well-stocked bar, not much drinking. They come to dance and that they do with great solemnity, not looking at each others' faces as they move around the floor, changing partners, teaching each other more complicated steps until midnight when the girls put their street shoes back on, kiss each other and everybody else goodbye and disappear into the night.

Viedma is on the Atlantic coast some five hundred miles to the south-east. I've come here to find a train to Ingeniero Jacobacci near the western border. Viedma is a holiday resort, usually calm and quiet. But today there's a demonstration in the streets, a group of bank workers, respectable middle-class white-collar workers, whose jobs are in jeopardy because the federal banks are going out of business and the workers are not being paid. A couple of hundred orderly men in suits and ties and their wives and children march to the Governor's mansion to voice their fears. But the Governor isn't about to make an appearance. He's probably left town and gone to his summer home.

Before leaving, I have lunch with a small group of railway men, union officials, hard-core Peronistas. They thought Menem was going to put into practice some of Perón's policies, but he has betrayed them.

At Ingeniero Jacobacci I switch to the Old Patagonian Express that goes south and now, at last, I am at the gateway to Patagonia. We move along through the deserted countryside – mile after mile of scrub and sand and a few settlements. There are some cows and horses and hundreds of dogs running wild, sometimes in packs, limping, some three-legged, with torn ears and battle scars on their backs.

The hills to the west grow into the snow-capped Andean foothills. Sometimes there's a run-down farm with a horse or two that stare at the train as it passes. And flocks of sheep which, being the stupidest of animals, run in panic from the train and the sound of its whistle, decades of experience of trains never leaving their tracks to menace them having made no impact on their tiny brains. Now and then a small pack of wild horses tries to outrun the train or race back and forth, kicking the air, like exuberant children with excess energy in their legs.

In El Maiten, I visit the repair station where old, sick and dying trains are cannibalized for their parts. They were going to close the repair station down, but the men who work here fought to keep it open and won at least a temporary reprieve. But it's hard to believe that, with lines shutting down every month, it can last much longer. The scene resembles a film from the twenties, with men banging away using tools that were obsolete decades ago.

The Old Patagonian Express runs on narrow-gauge tracks that make the train seem too delicate for the long journey down to Esquel. It seems like a big toy as it sways from side to side, steam and smoke spurting out of it into the clean, cold country air. Its journeys are now so infrequent that adults and kids

151

who live near the tracks come to stare at it and wave at the few passengers.

The old-fashioned wooden slat seats and the dining car with its Formica tables give it a quaint look. The attendants offer us ham sandwiches and little cakes and strong coffee in cups made in China on saucers made in Argentina.

Patagonia is vast and lonely – over three hundred thousand square miles from the Rio Colorado in the north-east to Tierra del Fuego in the south. Only four hundred thousand people live here, nearly half of them Chileans who cross the border to work the harvests. Patagonia got its name from Magellan who, when he discovered the place on his 1519 voyage, saw the fur- and hide-covered feet of the Indians and gave them the nickname of *Patagones* – people with big feet.

The locomotive uses an enormous amount of water. Now and then it stops to refill at a tank by the tracks but sometimes, when there's a drought, the tanks are empty and the train has to stop by a stream where the men will get off and hand-pump water through a hose.

I sit in the dining car with a man named Douglas Berwyn. Douggie's Welsh. That is to say, his great-grandparents were Welsh. In 1865 a group of 150 Welsh immigrants, escaping political repression and wanting to preserve their culture and language in a safe place, sailed to a beach in southern Patagonia. They went further west until they found land in the central Chubut region that they could cultivate. They wanted to create a 'Little Wales beyond Wales'. Although they got along very well with the Indians, they had an enormous struggle to stay alive in Patagonia's harsh and difficult climate. Other contingents of Welsh joined them over the years. They managed to keep their language alive for several generations, but now it's a losing battle.

The Welsh are sheep farmers and the market for wool has collapsed. The train passes by a huge *estancia* that belongs to the Benetton family. It's hard to imagine any of the Benettons leaving the lush beauty of the northern Italian countryside and coming to live in this part of the world where, among other things, the pasta is generally overcooked until it turns to paste. The local sheep farmers suspect that the Benettons are working on a plan to raise their own sheep for the wool they use, thus eliminating the need to buy from the local ranchers.

A Mapuche Indian, carrying his guitar, flags the train down in the middle of nowhere and climbs on. He starts playing and singing – songs in Mapuche and songs in Spanish – and some of the passengers join in with such enthusiasm that they almost miss their stop.

The Mapuches are spread throughout Patagonia. They came across the border from Chile. The train stops at a Mapuche settlement and he gets off. There are half a dozen old railroad worker shacks where the Mapuches live and run a small native craft shop – a room in which a group of old ladies work at looms. There is a bunch of little kids who seem to have nothing much to do but throw stones at the unhappy-looking dogs which dart back and forth, their tails between their legs, looking for a place to hide.

A few miles outside Esquel, the final stop, there's the town where Butch Cassidy, the Sundance Kid and the Kid's girlfriend, Etta Place, came to disappear. Their tale is so tangled now, so changed and improved on by local story-tellers, that it's hard to get straight. It seems that in 1902 the three of them sailed from the States to Buenos Aires, where they got another ship to the tip of Patagonia. They then rode on horseback up to Esquel where, using false names, they got a government land grant of several thousand hectares. They bought six thousand sheep, built a large, comfortable ranch house and tried to settle down. The local people said they always had plenty of money. They said the woman was a good shot. They said they were good neighbours.

But old habits die hard and, after a couple of banks were robbed and a Welshman was shot and an attempted kidnapping went awry, the Federales moved in. There was a shoot-out at the *estancia* where, the police claimed, Butch and Sundance were killed. Others say no – that they got away to Chile and were killed there, or that they just rode off and disappeared.

There are quite a few photographs showing the Cassidy bunch in front of their ranch house. Etta was quite beautiful. Sundance looked like a handsome college kid and Butch looked like a bar-room brawler, thick-faced and angry.

What's left of the *estancia* now is not much – a listing one-room shack where the present tenant lives with his two dogs, his chickens and his old horse.

OVERLEAF **The Old Patagonian Express runs when the fancy takes it, a wonderful toy-like anachronism in an age of bullet trains and jet travel**

His name is Aladino Sepúlveda and his quiet, inexpressive face is as weatherbeaten as the shack he has lived in for almost seventy years. There's a small corral and the remains of an outhouse. The only visible attempt at decor is an odd bit of landscaping – a row of empty green wine bottles stuck neck down in the dirt along the side of the shack. Aladino moves slowly and carefully and bears the curiosity of the occasional sight-seer with a quiet, possibly amused, dignity.

We have been riding straight down this deserted landscape for several hours, the Andes now high above us on both sides. I wonder why I see no animals moving. Douggie tells me that most of the animals are in the hills or are hiding – wild pig, ostriches, rabbits, foxes, even pumas that come down from the mountains at night to kill sheep. The eagles and hawks that wheel overhead from time to time are looking for roadkills or farm animals that have died.

And then, suddenly, the train moves down and passes through some green and fertile fields and finally into Esquel. Douggie offers to take me to a Welsh ranch in the hills above the city. He drives me there in his van, which is equipped with an array of electronic equipment. While he drives he's on the phone or cruising his ham radio band, while his tape deck blares out an endless chain of fifties rock, country and do-wop.

The ranch belongs to Mario Evans, a very big, powerful man, probably in his mid-forties. I have never felt quite this remote, standing on the land outside his house, the mountains towering above us. I have also never felt quite this cold. It's officially spring, but the vicious wind that whips off the Andes doesn't seem to know it.

Mario has a wife and a couple of sons who live mostly down below in the city. And he has a brother who sometimes works with him. But mostly he is alone up here. It seems a strange life for an apparently gregarious man with a lively sense of humour – but his father did it before him and, if he has his way, his sons will do it after he's gone. He wears a black poncho and beret, and chaps which he himself carved from the side of a cow. With his knife in his belt and his short whip like a cop's truncheon in his hand he rides off, his dogs racing to keep up, to hunt down one of the pumas that have been savaging his sheep. The image that Mario presents more clearly embodies the myth of the cowboy of a century ago than anyone I have ever seen before or probably ever will again.

There's not much to see in Esquel. But there's a cosy Welsh tea-house that serves a traditional high tea with scones and jam. And next to it is a small, plain church where I drop in to listen to the choir practise their Welsh hymns. They sing beautifully and very seriously, accompanied by a lady on an old harmonium operated by foot pedals. The strangeness of seeing these people singing in Welsh and then sitting down and gossiping in Spanish is almost a paradigm of Argentina itself – people from far away who have come to a strange, difficult land thousands of miles from the culture and civilization that formed them, making the best of a hard life with one foot tentatively in the past.

I would like to go further south, to Tierra del Fuego – the jumping-off point for visitors to the Antarctic – and the ports from which so many embarked and disappeared forever. But the train can go no further. The rails end here. The locomotive chugs on to a turntable, a short length of track on a trestle built over a pit, and two men turn the whole thing around by hand. I don't know how they do it. But in a few minutes the Old Patagonian Express is facing north.

London to Arkadia

TEXT BY RACHAEL HEATON-ARMSTRONG
ARCADIAN POEMS BY BEN OKRI

'Αρκαδία – from 'αρκω (avert, repulse, repel) and 'Αδης (Hades). The place where Hades is averted, i.e. immortality, as in Paradise.

Arkadia – a mountainous region in the central Peloponnese in southern Greece.

Arcadia – for over two thousand years a symbol in art, literature and philosophy; a place of pastoral simplicity, a lost paradise, Utopia.

WATERLOO STATION's elegance has been swamped by the inevitable flood of high street shops that provide everything except what you really need – the opportunity to sit and have a drinkable cup of coffee. In their determination to get to work on time frenzied commuters mow down holidaymakers either fleeing from or returning to their own stressful lives.

The Eurostar terminal is fifties space age streamline with a huge chrysalis-style glass roof which saunas its passengers in midsummer. In the international departure lounge people surge in fevered expectation of that moment when they can escape their outer world of announcements, cars, telephones, instructions, road drills, arguments, burglar alarms and banging doors. They step on to the train loaded with anticipation.

If you are lucky enough to travel first class you are served lunch by waiters whose accents entice you to France but whose uniforms anchor you firmly in England. The train meanders through the south London sprawl, saved from its usual drabness by late August's brilliant sun, past endless ribbons of red terraces whose occupants are sweltering in the hottest days for

'Let's meet under the clock': Ben Okri at Waterloo Station,
about to start his journey to Arkadia

twenty years, their Arcadian back gardens brimming with well-watered glory or burnt and worn bare by children chasing shadows.

There are a number of tunnels before *the one*, so when you do enter it you get no sense of being under water. It's not that you really expect to see the fishes, but . . .

After a short time in France it is announced that we are travelling at 300 kilometres an hour. If you look into the flat distance there is no feeling of speed, but try to focus on the bank and you'll sense a certain thrilling fear. The smoothness of the train is complemented by the vast open countryside in which rows of poplars stretch out like breakwaters between oceans of cropped corn. The scene is spotted with châteaux hidden behind ancient walls and surrounded by villages with tall-spired churches. Although most of the sunflowers have been harvested, those that still stand wave grandly in the breeze as we skim past.

Ben Okri, a Nigerian writer living in London, has long been interested in the idea of a lost paradise, a garden of Eden, a place of innocence to which we long to return. For two millennia the cultural symbol of this pastoral idyll has been Arcadia, which is also an actual place in the Peloponnese, the southern peninsula of Greece. Ben's route to Arcadia follows both the inner and outer journeys that people take to find this sanctuary of tranquillity.

Our first Arcadian was Jean-Luc, the driver of the Eurostar train on which we had travelled to France. He invited Ben back to his home on the outskirts of Paris. Although overshadowed by motorway flyovers and overhead railway lines, his garden still has the feel of a retreat. This suburban oasis is filled with well-loved flowers and trees which Jean-Luc and his wife have grown in the empty space into which they moved. Here they talked about their need both to work in and to enjoy their garden after busy days in the city. Oblivious to the traffic noise, they sit in perfect serenity that takes them back to the gardens of their childhood and the 'peace and nature' without which they could not survive.

The young Queen Marie Antoinette also needed to be reminded of her childhood in order to escape the strictures of the eighteenth-century French court and so, in the grounds of the Palais de Versailles outside Paris, she built L'Hameau. It is a perfect imitation of a farmyard, with barns and cottages, a mill with geraniums cascading over the balconies, and neat rows of grass on the thatched 'peasant-style' roofs. A gardener who lived in one of the cottages showed Ben his vegetables growing in rows as perfect as the grass ones on the roofs.

It was here that Marie Antoinette came to dress up and play the part of a shepherdess with her scented sheep. Although she never slept here, it gave her a few hours' respite from the formality of the court and an escape back into the innocence which she had only just left behind. She could not recapture her childhood, but she could be a child again. The imagined simplicity of life as a shepherdess was a perfect antidote to her duties as the King's wife.

Back in Paris, the Louvre is closed on Tuesdays, so that cleaners can clean and film crews can film. Outside, the incongruous glass pyramid still acts as a honeypot for the swarms of visitors. It is on these days that Pierre Rosenberg, the Louvre's flamboyant Director, finds his Utopia – when he can walk around the museum 'enjoying an image, singing to oneself, backwards, forwards, being able to escape from the everyday life, from the rumours of the city'. He spoke with pride of museums being for everyone the 'Arcadias in our day'.

We were here to look at the seventeenth-century artist Nicolas Poussin's *Les Bergers d'Arcadie*, in which a group of shepherds and a shepherdess are deciphering the words *'Et in Arcadia Ego'* inscribed on a tomb. The painting is one of the first to take up this theme, which originated in the poetry of the Greek writer Theocritus in the third century BC. Two centuries later, in his epic Latin poem the *Eclogues*, Virgil used the words as an inscription on the memorial of the shepherd Daphnis, lamenting his absence from the idyllic countryside in which he had once tended his flock. The painting's arid landscape of distant mountains and isolated trees is very similar to that of the real Arkadia, and very different from the lush valleys of Virgil's imagined Arcadia.

Ben had been introduced to the concept of Arcadia by Virgil, his favourite poet, and looking at this painting was a natural progression from that

OVERLEAF **Sleek trains in a streamlined terminal:
the Eurostar service awaits its next crowd of passengers**

interest. Ben talked about the possibility of it evoking a sense of humility – the idea that knowledge of death can increase one's capacity for happiness because of the realization of life's transience.

The explanation of the words *'Et in Arcadia Ego'* has long been open to discussion, and this is probably as Poussin would have wished it. Is death reminding the viewer that paradise is finite, or that paradise cannot exist without it? Or are we simply to acknowledge that all things must die or at least change their form? Its ambiguity leaves viewers to their own interpretations of the presence of death in Arcadia.

The gracious Gare de l'Est is the leaving point for Switzerland. As the train sped eastwards Ben spoke to a lady whose words were to be echoed throughout the journey. She suggested simply that travel teaches one to be at peace with oneself at home.

Whether it gives you peace or not, Switzerland has to be the most perfectly arranged country. Perfect fields, trees, crops, houses, bread, eggs, window boxes, beds, sheep, duvets – everything. Nature has been manicured – its wildness tamed, with the meadows so uniformly green that it is hard to imagine any cow being allowed to soil them. Every tiny piece of land is used – we even saw hay being made on the central reservation of a motorway. Most of the fields on the lower slopes are still scythed by hand by farmers whose lives are a far cry from the affluence and luxury of the cities. Switzerland is an enormously wealthy country where hard work and perseverance have created a totally organized structure, one of the few places in the world where you can be sure that the trains will run on time.

As the train doors opened, just over the border in Basel, the sweet Swiss air blew in and swept away the stuffiness of the carriage. Below the soupy, clouded sky a thick mist hung over the lakes, shrouding them in mystery. What had seemed so staged suddenly took on a whole new life, and nature once more reigned supreme.

Our first stop in Switzerland was the Goetheanum, named after Germany's most illustrious writer and thinker – a huge and imposing concrete mushroom that looms high above the town of Arlesheim. Designed by Rudolf Steiner to replace his wooden original – thought to have been burnt down by the local Catholics, who felt threatened by the new ideas it represented – the building was not completed until 1928, three years after his death. Steiner had spent many years editing Goethe's scientific work, which reinforced his own experiences of harmonizing the spiritual world with the natural one. These beliefs were to be the foundation of the Anthroposophical Society which Steiner founded in 1913, in the hope that his work involving architecture, dance and art, in schools, communities for the handicapped, banks and many different businesses, would lead to the forging of new relationships between people and the planet.

The Goetheanum is the nerve centre of the Steiner movement, where anthroposophists come for seminars, eurhythmics is danced in joy and followers walk around in awe. It is a place of enormous power which manages to be both authoritarian and creative. With no straight lines, and staircases that seem to float into each other, it has an air of wild genius, creating in visitors the desire either to flee or to stay forever. Steiner was a great visionary who taught ways to 'go into civilization without fear', where 'only he who understands life can become a truly practical man' – to embrace the modern world of technology and bring spirituality into it.

In the new stained glass-windowed theatre a production of Goethe's *Faust* is regularly performed to explore these ideas. Goethe saw Arcadia not as a destination in itself, but as a stage of consciousness that Faust – and humankind – can visit and then carry with them to enhance their inner strength on the continuing journey through the material world.

Here Ben met the company's leading actor and director, Georg Darvas, whose travelling in recent years has brought him fresh rewards – rewards that were a reflection of the ones which Ben had had whilst looking at the mountains that morning. For both of them, becoming inwardly quiet allows the nature and the history of a place to speak and bring spiritual resurgence. It is not something that can be searched for, but it may happen in the open stillness of meditation. On the future of humanity Darvas says 'We have to go through things like war for a long time because you can't convince the masses that there's a spiritual world. Our movement can never be a mass one . . . you have to conquer yourself individually.'

The Camphill Movement was founded on the teachings of Steiner, with the intention of creating communities where mentally handicapped people could live with co-workers who share the daily tasks. Ideally, each person contributes what he or she can towards the well-being of the other members and the group as a whole. There are three Camphills in Switzerland, and we visited one in the centre of the country near Worb. The enormous garden is full of carefully tended flowers, vegetables and plump fruits, all watched over by the surrounding mountains.

Johanna and Hans Spalinger, who founded Humanus Haus here and are building another one in Romania, are a rare couple whose fulfilment lies in helping other people to have self-respect, to be happy and to follow their own destiny. They have created an atmosphere of warmth and delight, which supplies energy and strength. Those who work here have a talent for giving and understanding, which is in turn fed by the people whom they look after.

Ben was introduced to Rita, who is well enough to sleep at her parents' house but spends her days here weaving and playing the piano. She played Bach in the centre of the big empty hall – pink from paint made from crushed coral and the afternoon light – and created such magic that all our silenced emotions were turned inside out and left brimming with hope. When Rita is feeling stressed she listens to music or plays it herself; either way it brings her a sense of calm and relief.

Everyone in the community works – not for money, but because they enjoy doing it for other people – and everything that is made is either used or sold in the shop. Here are beautifully made things from Camphills all over the world – glasses, clothes, toys, cards, lyres, stools, mugs, candles, wind chimes, carvings, xylophones, ornaments, calendars, napkins . . . .

At Humanus Haus cloth is made right from the first stage of carding the fibres, through spinning, dyeing and finally to weaving. Ben was guided through a weaving lesson by Clemens, who has spent some time in England. He is intelligent and well-read, and loves to paint and write and talk of cabbages and kings. Bread, too, is made from its organic beginning: the corn is grown on the farm, threshed, ground and baked. Everyone does the job that suits them best. One lady has to keep on the move because she is diabetic, so she does all

Ben Okri reads as the train passes through the tidy conformity that is Switzerland

the deliveries around the village and can be seen darting around with baskets of provisions. The farm animals are of great value to some of the residents – particularly to one girl, who is normally very withdrawn and fearful but goes, in secret, at dawn each day to stroke and talk to the usually unapproachable bull. Places such as Humanus Haus are a brave and far-sighted attempt to create modern-day Arcadias.

From Zurich we took the panoramic train south over the Alps and into Italy. The train's windows are extra-large and stretch above your head, so the untamed mountains can prove that they at least have escaped Swiss precision. Once we are over the St Gotthard Pass the lakes are no longer pale and mysterious but are brilliant blue reflections of the sky. The atmosphere changes – unkempt fields, peeling paint and cars left to rust. Beauty here is allowed to live and breathe.

Coming into Milan the train passes the magnificent cathedral, newly cleaned and brilliant in its pinnacled beauty. Home of the stock exchange and of the country's best shops and restaurants, the city is more business-like than any other in Italy. The world's leading centre for design, it is brimming with elegant, well-dressed people for whom making a *bella figura* is vital even when nipping out for a loaf of bread.

Milan's most celebrated author, publisher and lover of Greece and her history, Roberto Calasso, talked to Ben about the clichéd image of the tranquillity of nature. In ancient times the Arkadian people were reputed to be the most boorish and blasphemous in Greece and this, together with the inhospitable landscape, makes a strange bed for the image of peace and serenity to lie on. However, without this enigmatic character the theme becomes 'rather insipid and boring and a useless, lifeless background in your mind'. And everyone knows that nature is neither simple nor innocent. Roberto spoke of the last stage of life and thought – what the ancient Indians called the forest thought, the doctrine of the forest: 'It has to do with what is wild and the divine quality of the wilderness.' He suggested that we tend to be scared of what is wild in the belief that it comes before thought, whereas wildness is actually beyond thought. The Indians knew that they 'had to extract a sort of thought from that forest without which the tame world would become totally sterilized'.

As the train rumbles over the causeway into Venice the sunset warms the city pink. The threat of disappointment – that it may not be as lovely as the Cornetto adverts, that it will be packed with tourists, that there will be cars, that it will smell – is averted immediately, for it is extraordinarily beautiful. A working city of homes, markets, schools, restaurants, shops, churches, offices and tourists like any other, it is nevertheless preserved by its own nature. There is physically no room for cars and visually no space for hoardings.

During the day delivery-boats piled high make their way to and fro, bus-boats pack on too many commuters, fire-boats scream round corners, their heroes' hair swept back in the spray, tour-boats carry holidaymakers in matching baseball caps to buy coloured glass and masks – and life goes on. The city fathers have managed to protect Venice from neon and McDonald's, and receive money from UNESCO in an attempt to slow down further crumbling. It remains a curious mixture of the sublime and the ridiculous, with heritage the victor. At the end of the day cats squabble in alleys and the evening light throws perfect reflections on the stilling waters. Occasionally the quiet is splintered by an over-painted gondola taking awe-struck Japanese on a piped music cruise.

A typical Venetian, Rozella Zorza is a professor of English and American Studies who loves her city. She explained to Ben how many people whose creativity has run low have visited Venice and found that 'the peace of the place is such that they can find their new voice again'. For her it is a city of presences made up of the artists and writers who have described it and enabled it to be seen in a different way. It is in reading and looking at these people's work that she can enter an enclosed space and for a while forget the outside world – not to escape it, but to have a 'little pause'. Ben and Rozella discussed the '*Et in Arcadia Ego*' theme in relation to looking at something very beautiful and wonderful, knowing that it will be destroyed or will decay – that death will reach it in one way or another.

The tragedy in former Yugoslavia has made it almost impossible to get the train all the way to Greece, so we took one down the east coast of Italy in order to

OVERLEAF **Milan Station, gateway to an elegant and affluent city**

catch the ferry from Brindisi. It is a twelve-hour journey past endless rows of umbrellas, sunbeds and holidaying families – about 600 miles of warm flat sea stared at by cement blocks of hotels and apartments. Two wide-eyed children gleefully told Ben of their personal paradises. For one it was the Italian funfair Luna Park, and for the other 'a country with only children, with clouds instead of stones and everything with wings like angels'.

We passed through the industrial wasteland surrounding Bari, the capital of the south – as bleak as the view that is sometimes found in struggling eastern Europe, with acre upon acre of concrete chicken-coop housing. The whole area is broken down, as if it had been deserted many years ago and reinhabited in the sixties and seventies by strangers scraping together bits of land in between the rubbish. Bari is the entry point for many economic refugees from North Africa and has become a place of unemployment, crime and disappointed dreams. Even on a brilliant summer's day the air is stagnant with fumes and frustrations. At least the sea can help to heal these boxed people when they lie spread-eagled on the beach.

In the midst of the endless flat coastal plain we spent a day in the medieval town of Ostuni. Like an oasis on the only hill for miles, it was deserted by all but ghosts and memories until a short time ago. Now lured back to life by restorers' visions, it is a brilliant white maze of circling stairs and disappearing alleys. The windowframes' blue matches the cloudless sky under which this picture-book town hides its secrets.

Brindisi has the excitement of a large port filled with travellers and sailors out for a good time. There is a struggle here similar to that of Bari, but infused with hope and purposeful transience. We were there on St Theodore's Day, when the town was awash with stalls selling ice cream, carvings, sweets, beads, toys, semi-cured leather goods, colouring books and all kinds of multicoloured tat to widen the eyes of children. In the midst of all this, in a park usually picnicked in by families waiting for the ferry, Ben mused over a statue of Virgil sadly distinguished only by its graffiti. An attempt to pay homage to this great poet and propagator of the Arcadian myth, it shows him as an angel surrounded by images from his works – a helmet, a horse and a lamb.

Being late in the season, the overnight crossing from Brindisi to the Greek port of Patras is quiet and peaceful, with only a handful of backpackers sleeping on deck. Just before dawn the darkness of Ithaca emerges from the sea, and as we slowly pass it the rising sun brings the island into focus. Known primarily as the place where Penelope waited ten years for the return of her husband, Odysseus, it was also written about by the Greek poet Constantine Cavafy, who was himself an exile, born in Egypt. In the freshness of the dawn Ben met Emilios Bourantinos, on his way home to Greece, whose knowledge about mythology led them into discussions about Cavafy's poem 'Ithaca'. In it he uses the island and its history as a symbol for the importance of experiencing the journey rather than the arrival. The final destination may seem a disappointment, but the experience and knowledge gained along the way will always more than compensate.

The Greek Tourist Board is trying to promote the Peloponnese – to spread the wealth from the over-packaged islands and to stop the exodus to America that the region is known for. The tides are slowly turning – probably not because of tourism, however, but because the young are returning from their adoptive lands to find an easier way of life in a place where you can walk the streets at night and leave your house unlocked. In a bar in Tripolis, the capital of Arkadia, we talked to a number of young people with perfect American accents and slick American fashions, who have reacted to their parents' escape by coming back. The search for, and return to, Arkadia spirals on.

The elderly train follows the coast east from Patras along the Gulf of Corinth towards Athens. We passed Egio, where some months earlier an earthquake had ripped through the town in the middle of the night and killed twenty-six people. The people here live in constant fear, and with it a kind of hopeful resignation.

On the train was a mixture of Greeks on business attempting coolness in first class; venerable black-dressed and hair-dyed women nestled comfortably in fat from childbearing, surrounded by bulging carrier bags on the hard bench seats; eager backpackers seeking adventure among the ruins; fresh-faced soldiers returning home for R & R; a high-hatted priest saying his rosary; two middle-aged women, still drunk from the night before, who laughed and sang and kissed Ben on both cheeks and asked if he was married; and old men. The

ABOVE Near Tripolis, in the heart of geographical Arkadia

OPPOSITE The guard at Corinth Station

most popular game for older men in Greece is 'Let's go down to the coffee shop and shout'. The carriages ring with their bellowing voices. Every now and then the train stops in the middle of nowhere for someone to get on or off, or for the single-track points to be changed by a heavy-levered hand.

At Corinth we change on to a smaller and more modern train. Brilliant red and blue, it has only two carriages and is more like a suburban city train than the kind you would expect to cross mountains. It will take us south along the coast, where we will stop to make a visit, then turn inland for its final destination: Tripolis, in the heart of Arkadia.

Mary and Elias' taverna on the Bay of Argolis is blissfully hidden away from the usual tourist route. On the edge of the sea, it is surrounded by the hot tranquillity of olive groves.

Mary Kelly has the soft strength of an earth-mother without the earnest sandals. She sat with Ben and told him how she left her home in Ireland to spread her wings in Germany, where she ran a successful business and led a driven city life. After years of fighting to be herself within the strictures of German society, she came here to the Arkadian coast where she found Elias. She hadn't been looking for somewhere new, but when she arrived she knew it was the fulfilment of a dream she had never had. She still runs a business as well as the taverna, and brings up their three children, but with Elias 'who has the means to make something idyllic – he just lives his life and never worries about tomorrow and never cries about yesterday' her destiny has been found.

Their children have a freedom that would be impossible in most European countries, and Mary believes this gives them the strength and independence they will need in later life. A lasting image was her description of the Greek christenings which are often held by the sea here. The child is completely immersed in local olive oil and is not allowed to be washed until three days after the ceremony. The christening robe must then be rinsed in the sea before being washed with soap. Although Mary had had her reservations, her own daughter was christened in this way. For some days afterwards the child was completely serene.

Back on the little train which slowly creeps up into the uncultivated wilderness, past drowsy station cafés filled with coffee-sipping men, we look out on a landscape gradually becoming harder and wilder. The red roofs and multicoloured flowers of the village-sprinkled hills give way to bleached valleys and tall mountains as the railway line dips between slopes dyed crimson with manganese deposits. Eagles circle high above the skylarks. There is a sense of leaving something behind, of going somewhere magical. This is the land where the Evil Eye can wreak havoc, where the following year's weather can be forecast from the clouds in the first week of August, where shepherds still pipe homage to Pan and where fortunes can be told from the shoulder bone of a lamb. It is a place seldom visited and little known.

We arrived in the heart of the Arkadian mountains to meet Harilambus, whom we found asleep under a huge and ancient oak tree. His goats were some distance away, guarded by tame dogs which live with them as protection from the feral dogs which attack the young kids. As gently as Harilambus awoke, so did the goats, which slowly wandered towards their watering-place. The sound of their bells rings through the valley every day as they follow their morning sleep with a drink before going up the mountain again to graze. At the beginning of the summer they are given the season's haircut – cropped sides to keep cool, and an uncut strip along the spine to prevent sunburn. But these punk goats maintain their dignity with a wild array of different-shaped horns and posture that would grace kings.

Harilambus was born in America and lived there for his first ten years. His father, Yannis, had gone in search of new horizons and made a good living working in restaurants, but he found he was not enjoying city life and did not want to bring up his children with American values. He needed to return to his roots and the life to which he was born – the life of a shepherd, which he had started to learn at the age of two.

Now twenty-three, Harilambus has the choice to leave. When the snow is so heavy that it suffocates the trees and the branches break under its weight; when the animals need feeding, watering and constant attention; when the days are lonely and dark and the silence is bone-freezing – these are the times when America beckons. But sunny afternoons that warm the brilliant yellow crocuses and the comfort of a small goat nestling into his siesta make leaving an impossibility again. For the moment he is content to wait for the sign of an angel.

Arcadian Poems by Ben Okri

A woman and her donkey near Tripolis in Arkadia

OPPOSITE Herding goats in modern Arkadia, just as it was in Virgil's
time two thousand years ago

PAGE 186 An old woman working in the fields among 'the rough-scrub skin
of wild serene Arkadia'

COMING TO ARCADIA

If you're coming to Arcadia
You must bring something with you
You must bring a gift
Worthy of the gods
That rest in mountains and in songs.

Don't bring seven silk parasols
Or a diamond ring
With seven stones
Or a mandolin for a land
That's rich with the music of Pan.

Nor must you bring yourself alone
For what you are is not yet the great gift
But an offering which Arcadia
Might perfect into one.

And don't just bring the self
That you live with every day;
Bring the selves that you've
Forgotten, the selves
That live and grow in play.

2
Your gift must be rare.
It must be the blood and craft
Of your life's most suffered strivings.

It must be the essence
Of what you have made
From rocks and sunlight and time.

It must be the balsam
And tough fruit that shepherds pulp
As offerings on the divine altar.

3
Your gift must be
Stranger than love
Richer than suffering
Deeper than death
Riper than happiness

And vaster than the circling
Seas around the mountains
Which are really the forms
Of the sleeping and mighty dead.

Your gift must be one that
Shines through the night of ages
And soothes the traveller
In the storms and lowered thunder

And one that keeps the heart
Of the child
Forever alive
In a world that dies
With each circling of the distant sun.

If you're coming to Arcadia
You must bring something with you –
A little star that grows and shines
Beyond the tears and laughter of the shrines.

DEPARTURE FROM WORB (FOR JONATHAN)

The mountains all alive;
The roseate intensities over silver peaks;
A deer on the community's field;
And solitary trees on flat plains.

The driver speeding, one hand on wheel;
And the two practical dreamers
Of Humanus Haus, linked arm in arm,
Walking gently, heads bowed,
Returning to their great and humbling
Task, while we carried on
Our quest for other arcadias.

I remember the sun-heated swimming pool;
The cattle and sheep on the other fields;
The villagers going about their measured
Tasks; Edward with his stylish hat.

I remember Humanus Haus;
With its name based on the unfinished
Novel by Goethe, called *The Secret*,
Which is about the future guides of humankind.

I dream now of the soft edges
Of door-corners and buildings;
Architecture, Hans said, should show
On its outward forms
The activities going on inside:
As within, so without.

There should be spaces before portals
And doorways to prepare our spirits
For entry; doors shouldn't be square,

But inviting; they shouldn't be aggressive,
And should call the visitant to quiet mysteries.

I dream of colour-schemes on stained-glass
Windows, with initiations and deaths
Into higher individual realms.
There should always be calm spaces
Before doorways so that the entrant
Has their being prepared
For the higher activities beyond.

Novels ought to have initiatory openings
That prepare you for higher dreaming.
There should also be interior architecture:
High ceilings which soothe and free
The spirit, freeing stress, enabling
The best self within to soar
And guide the man or woman:
Spaces that mirror your own inner infinity.

There should be unique spaces
Within buildings and art which make
Music heard much clearer.

In the world before birth, Hans said,
When you look down on earth
You see many lights, many arcadias,
In different places. And one day,
A long way in the future, those brightly lit
Places will link hands and come together.

And then an ascent towards
A new golden age can begin.

OSTUNI (FOR ROSEMARY AND BRENDA)

Your white houses clustered on the hill
Are tight as a fortress.
They look down from their cubist forms
And they hide your sea of olives
On the plains of green behind
That rides down shimmering
With dark shadows
Into the flat calm of the Adriatic.

I love your old town
With its Moorish moods
And moody side streets that
Vanish into whiteness;
And your peaceful skylines
And your domed modest churches
Of Byzantine melodies.

I am haunted by your allotments
Where the women work and age
In the green ages;
And your empty central quarters
And your rising streets,
Hidden and mysterious.

Do you dream of your fringed fortress
And high walls
And your lights on the high hill
Brilliant at night,
Alone in the dark?

I think often of your woven air
Of siestas and unfinished dreams
And your history of being conquered
And absorbing your conqueror's moods

Into your sleeping freedom;
And your cathedral
Where old women sit on the stairs
Waiting for the priest to open
The ancient purple doors
And your squares, awaiting visitors,
Staring down at a world
Of dwindling infinities.

All these things rise to me
In your ochre and white syllables.
They whisper of a hidden sea
And places where one ought
To set out from
But where a blessed woman
Offered mandorla to a stranger
And accepted from him a token,
An orange, a stranger's gratitude
For warmth.

There lingers in that woman's eyes
The sensual dawn
Of a town on a hill
A town that should be weightless
In flight beyond the Adriatic
But which lies enclosed
In history's dreaming walls.

Surrounded by garments of olive leaves
Under a sky limned with blue
Let your unfinished dreams
Be touched by God's infinite shape
And become more than just
An enamel bowl of escape.

VIRGIL IN BRINDISI

He drifted into harbour
Lying in state
When the wine-drenched sea
Was clear as a slate;

He dreamt of his great poem
Restless in him unfinished
And wept that twelve years
Beyond death were needed
For its perfection to be undiminished.

The great emperor vertical
On another ship
Against a changing imperial sky
Could never have guessed
That in his poet's unrest
An eternal world would soar high.

PATRAS
(WHERE I WAS MADE STATION-MASTER FOR AN HOUR)

O stones of the harbourfront
Where love mingles with mountain
And the tranquil blue-mint sea.

Your old city up in the heights
Doesn't envy the new.
That is how the old gods dream:
Retreating into the stones,
Away from the blustering cars
And the new ships from Egypt
Out of whose painted mouth of metal
Stream the hump-backed travellers
Who wander your streets,
Searching for ancient carnivals.

Old gods in giving way to the new
Hide themselves deeper
Into the infolding earth
That was once a powerful sea
Where Poseidon's trident stirred
Undercurrents of the tragic muse.

But the ancient theatres
And creative vines
Are resting now from centuries
When the gods interpenetrated
The unbridled dreams of men.

Sunlight lies blessed
On the small new gods
Sweltering in the moods
Of an exhausted mine.

Such lands can't stay blessed forever:
Lands favoured by gods
Often pay with parched time –
While civilization roars downward
With funicular trains
And the misted air of modern pollutions.

And now dignified men with walking sticks
And stoic women in whom Greek genius
Lies slumbering like the red flowers
And the rounded figs
And the old women with black shawls
At crossroads
Watch the trains rattling over a dry
Earth, unimpregnated by the old gods.

O ancient city of the blue-mint sea
Have you forgotten that the mountains
Shrouded in rich mists of silver
Still hide the mystery of the hidden ones?

O stones of the harbourfront
You alone hear the laughter
In the invisible rain from above;
But to us you sing now a siesta song,
Of golden poverty, and love.

Mountains all around.
Secret springs so cold in winter
That even the goats can't drink.
And snow three feet high
In the white season.

In the old days shepherds,
Transmuting loneliness and hard
Work, sang songs to one another;
Sang of love, and lost love,
And exile; and indulged in songs
Of alternating voices.
They sang the origin of things,
They sang of Pan, and of Silenus,
And of a new golden age
Initiated by the birth
Of a miraculous child;
They sang of death,
And the beech tree's shade;
They sang of love conquering all.

Now the shepherds don't sing any more.
They compete; they quarrel;
They are suspicious of one another;
And they have to pay taxes
To the church, and the neighbouring villages
For feeding the goats.
Mountains belonging to the earth
Belong now to churches.

And a shepherd who has returned from exile
Now wrestles with the harsh
Beauty of the mountains.
And his son, lean and blessed
With unnatural shepherd's grace,
A grace that ancient heroes
Might have envied,
Is now torn between the hardship
Of the flock,
The hard love of nurturing
The goats, the rugged love
That Arcadia demands,
And the dreams of going away
To famous and corrupting cities,
A dream of initiation into
The world's true realities,
The dream of becoming
A man in an unfamiliar
Unarcadian world.

And we in the soul-diminishing world
Crave the serenity of his Arcadia.

There is unease
In all Arcadias.

Mountains all around.
Crocuses and cyclamen
On the dry patches of rock
And stony beauty.
Shadows of clouds
Like juggernauts over
The peaks that we can't live on.
A solitary church
On the remote heights.
And wild dogs, previously tame,
Fled or let loose from the cities:
They have returned
To the sleeping wildness within them,
And turned half-wolf,
And ravage the sheep
And the bell-following goats.

Inaccessible beauty all around;
A beauty that disdains
Your heart or your love.
A wild deity, forgotten
And no longer celebrated in song,
Presides over this ferocious
Beauty of a wild-hearted woman
Who resembles the gods
That were before the gods
And who is too stony and severe
For the watery loves of men.

A harsh beauty all around;
And the haunting bells
As the mountain quivers

When the goats, bell-led by rams and
A stony-horned and baggy-scrotumed
Leader, wend their eerie way
Down the mountain paths –
Paths they have created
With their single-file chewing.

The mountain silence resonates
With the bells and the odd cries
Of the shepherd and the fleet-footed
Movements of his son
And the soft murmurs of the wind
That so vainly tries to rouse
The heart and soothe the rough-scrub
Skin of wild serene Arkadia.

And over the mountains
A giant head suddenly appears,
Dark and monstrous
Like an angry god
Or like one of the forgotten giants
That tried to climb Mount Olympus
To the Olympians'
Newly tranquil home.

Giant shadow of giant head
Over the mighty mountain.
And the world all around
Goes still, in fright,
Under a primeval enchantment.
The giant head moves,
And grows mightier.

Then an even greater pair
Of shoulders, made of the shadow
Of another world, like an
Unnatural colossus,
Moves over the peaks.
Greater and greater
The form appears,
Till the world fears that
Pan, long abolished by the cross,
Again prowls the mysterious
Peaks of Arkady.

And then the gigantic form
Occupies the mountain,
Becomes its bulk,
And dissolves
Into the dissolving
Radiance of the sun.
And then, under an assault
Of clouds, the mountains move,
As they once did,
When the gods made the earth
Their hunting-ground of love
Their play-ground of heroic
Human tragedies.

Arcadia remains tranquil;
It hides its powers, myths,
Wildernesses, its beauty,
Dangers, and its madness
Within the simple hopes
We bring to it, fired by
A poet's dream of old.

And Arcadia remains a fantasy,
And a dream, best found
In the hearts and thoughts
Of humanity, a redeeming
Oasis from an ever-fragmenting
World, a cool secret spring,
Never attainable, but cooler
Than the most soothing thing.
It is much needed
Under life's tough sunlight.

Arcadian stillness all around.
Arcadian stillness remains.
Its dream grows.
Its dream grows best
For those who know
The fire within wonder
And who work secretly
For a new golden age
Remade from that eternal
Human longing
For a human way
Of perfection.

The calm mountains call us.
And within the prowling
Silent gods
Of our dreams
Arcadia lingers
And calls to us –
In this age
Of fire without love.

FAREWELL TO ARCADIA

You have arrived and now you depart
To the old places with a stronger heart

You have travelled the world's ever-surprising tracks
And met many with strange destinies on their backs

You have borne much on the great road
And love has always lightened your load

You have passed an old woman with a scythe
And nodded to her, your love of life as magic tithe

You have listened to the obscure women of fate
And they have taught you to live with joy, and not to hate

And so you take to the hidden way
To where you can grow and deepen and play

And so you go up to the mythic mountains
To replenish in the healing fountains

The higher places are the best for you
That's where the heart is free, and true

But you return now to the world where you must live
The world is the best place to learn and give

You have arrived and now you depart
With a wiser and stronger heart.

Great Zimbabwe to Kilimatinde

HENRY LOUIS GATES JR

'Well . . . a week ago when I left home, I was an African American. Now, I'm just an American.'   LIZA GATES

'Before I came to Kilimatinde, I didn't even know that the Wagogo people existed. Now I am one!'   MAGGIE GATES

I FIRST VISITED AFRICA a quarter of a century ago. I had become fascinated by it in the fifties while watching Saturday children's programmes, serials such as *Ramar of the Jungle* and *Sheena, Queen of the Jungle*, as well as the now classic kitsch films such as *King Kong, Mighty Joe Young, Tarzan* and *Zulu*. While I sometimes found their depictions of Africans unpleasant and demeaning, nothing could interfere with the allure that this continent of black people and its wonderfully strange animals had for me.

Why Africa? I have thought about this often and for a very long time. Certainly my attitudes towards the continent were not typical of those held within my family and among my friends, growing up in the darkest years of the Civil Rights movement during the mid- to late 1950s. The Negro Americans I knew used to make disparaging remarks about Africans that were often as offensive as those made by white Americans. 'I ain't left nuthin' back in Africa,' the old saying would go. 'Nothing but your soul,' Malcolm X would respond a few years later: 'Your soul and your names.' It was as if Negroes in

Henry Louis Gates outside the village of Kilimatinde in Tanzania, where as a student he worked in a mission hospital

191

America felt themselves to be the vanguard of the African peoples – a commonly voiced opinion before 1957, the year of Ghana's independence, even by those who should have known better, such as Richard Wright or W. E. B. Du Bois – and as if we needed the Africans, 'benighted' by the jungle and colonialism, as something of a baseline of blackness against which to measure ourselves. No matter how bad things were in America, we seemed to reason, things were not as bad here as they were in darkest Africa. Richard Pryor, on a comedy album based on his first trip to the continent, summed up this attitude with the words: 'Thank God for slavery.'

I did not share this attitude, despite the fact that I was as eager to be a member of the great American middle class as any of my relatives or contemporaries. I can't say why, but the great year of African independence, 1960, captured my imagination as few other public events had done. Only the Civil Rights movement loomed as large. I even memorized the names of the new nations' presidents and prime ministers, and, all too soon, their military juntas and strong men.

At about this time, *Reader's Digest* featured a story about an African boy who had *walked* thousands of miles across the continent, hoping desperately to come to America to be educated. I read the piece over and over again: yes, he had *walked*, through bush and jungles, up mountains and across deserts, all to get to America. And there he was, starring up at me from page fifty-nine of *Reader's Digest*, having walked across Africa, been adopted by missionaries, then sent to the States to attend school. (He had been so filthy from his journey, I recall, that the missionaries had forced him to bath three times in a row before allowing him to try on his new clothes!) Here this boy was, risking his life to come all the way to America, and I found myself wanting desperately – at the age of ten – to go the other way.

Then, too, there was the call of the inimitable Dr Livingstone. Geography class, which I loved, was full of tales of the great explorers: Marco Polo, Vasco da Gama, Pizarro, Ponce de León, Henry the Navigator – the list was long and noble. But none rivalled David Livingstone's adventures in Africa. For me, Livingstone's passionate campaign against slavery, his ardent love of the mystery and vastness of the continent and its sheer diversity of peoples, plants and creatures, his determination to bring 'Civilization, Commerce and

Christianity' even to the darkest southern and East African interior regions about which the West knew virtually nothing, were irresistibly compelling.

What fictional story could ever rival the adventure of Livingstone's 'discovery' of Victoria Falls for the white world, his desperate search for the source of the Nile, his mistaken belief that he *had* discovered it, his fever-induced delirium of prayers of thanks to God for allowing him to make this discovery, his death on his knees during one of those very prayers? And, as if this were not enough to fire any schoolboy's imagination with visions of pith helmets, caravans, elephants, lions and hyenas, there was the noble act of Livingstone's two faithful servants, who – following their master's command – had cut out his heart and buried it in Africa, salted and dried his body in the sun, then carried it in a hollow log for nine months from today's Zambia all the way to Bagamoyo in today's Tanzania, where it was shipped back to London for a state funeral in Westminster Abbey! Now *that* was some story. Between the passion of that African boy whose face peered up at me from the pages of *Reader's Digest*, and Livingstone's fearless ambition to reveal the mysteries of the Nile, how could a curious little coloured boy from the village of Piedmont, West Virginia resist Mother Africa's lure?

I read avidly about Africa – as avidly as a high school student in Appalachia could read. Albert Schweitzer at Lambaréné, heads of state emerging from the Kennedy White House, the crisis over Katanga province, Lumumba's assassination, Mobutu's brutal triumph against democracy, the coup against Nkrumah ending an era of optimism that was all too painfully brief, the murders at Sharpeville, Mandela's imprisonment, Kip Keino's victory at the Olympics – all of this was Africa to me.

Yale, where I became an undergraduate in 1969, sponsored one of those sixties programmes that sent students to work for a year in the Third World immediately following their sophomore (second) year. The sole stipulation of the scheme, called 'The Five-Year BA', was that an applicant should secure em-ployment rather than study abroad at a university, like the typical 'junior-year abroad' programmes that regularly send students to Britain, France, Greece or Spain. Long past the deadlines for applications – in fact, long after the twelve finalists had been selected – I was able to persuade a sensitive dean at Yale that a year in Africa, structured around the idea of work and travel, would be a meaningful part of my larger education.

Somewhat amused at my determination, I believe, and somewhat sympathetic to the thick anti-war atmosphere that was just beginning to engulf our campus, the dean relented, found most of the necessary funds and granted me leave of absence as well as quasi-status as a member of the programme. I, for my part, raised the remainder of the money for my air fare by writing to churches and civic groups, like the Lions Club in my home town, and secured a job through the good graces of the Bishop of the Episcopal Diocese of the State of West Virginia. Our school year culminated in a strike by both students and faculty members in protest at the war in Vietnam.

The Anglican Communion, as it is called, is structured, in part, around the pairing of diocese in the First World with those in the Third World. As luck would have it, the 'sister' of the Diocese of West Virginia was the Diocese of Central Tanganyika. At the time it was still headed by an expatriate, a missionary from Australia. Our diocese had sent donations quite regularly to Tanzania; now, it seems, it was ready to send me, having recently received a black church official from Tanzania who encouraged this sort of exchange.

Tanzania could not have been a more perfect choice. Not only had so many of us become enamoured of its president, Julius Nyerere (who held a master's degree from Edinburgh and had translated *Hamlet* into Swahili), but I was eager to witness the workings of the Tanzanian version of 'African socialism', through Nyerere's *Ujamaa* policy (the creation of villages). Nyerere and his compatriots had declared *Ujamaa* to be based upon traditional economic institutions indigenous to a collective and communal black African past. By the spring of 1970 Yale – and all America – had become engulfed in the politics of black nationalism, the FBI's brutal repression of the Black Panthers, and the dramatically swelling numbers of students and faculty members adamantly opposed to the war in Vietnam.

Whether capitalism could ever adequately accommodate the economic integration of African Americans was a question very much on our minds.

**The Victoria Falls on the Zambezi River, more descriptively known as
'Mosi-oa-Tunya' or 'the smoke that thunders'**

The opportunity to live in a black socialist country would enable me to see for myself if what Mao Zedong had called the great experiment with human nature could actually work. And over-riding even this concern was that of the relationship that Africans in the New World – specifically our people – bore to those in the Old World. Countee Cullen, the great black poet of the Harlem Renaissance, had addressed this perennial quandary in his widely anthologized poem 'Heritage':

> What is Africa to me?
> Spicy grove and cinnamon tree.

Malcolm X, consistent with his black nationalist politics, had answered Cullen's rhetorical question with a bold affirmation of linkage: 'What made us feel helpless,' he argued, 'was our hatred for ourselves. And our hatred of ourselves stemmed from our hatred for things African.' Martin Luther King, on the other hand, had taken the opposite position: 'The Negro is an American,' he had declared just as firmly as Malcolm X had the converse. 'We know nothing of Africa. He's got to face the fact that he is an American.' My own determination to go to Africa reflected my desire to come to terms with this question myself.

When the BBC approached me about participating in this series, I couldn't believe the accident of timing and my good luck. A quarter of a century earlier I had made what I thought of as my first pilgrimage to Africa. It had included six months in the village of Kilimatinde, the home of an Anglican mission hospital where I was trained to deliver general anaesthesia and where I lived and worked with Australian missionaries. This was followed by two months of hitch-hiking right across the Equator, from Dar es Salaam on the Indian Ocean to the mouth of the Congo River on the Atlantic Ocean, through Tanzania, Kenya, Uganda, Rwanda and straight through the massive expanse of the Congo. Now, twenty-five years later, I found myself offered the chance to return with a camera crew to encounter that region, as well as my much younger self, all over again.

Of course I would do it! But I had three conditions: that the train journey should unfold in southern and eastern Africa; that it should end in the village of Kilimatinde; and that my wife, Sharon Adams, and our two daughters,

Maggie, aged fifteen, and Liza, aged thirteen, should present the television programme alongside me. The BBC, after much debate and deliberation, agreed to give my curious scheme a try. My family, for its part, had curiously mixed emotions.

Sharon, as is her wont, leaped into the preparations with unbounded enthusiasm, obtaining travel guides, art books and information on the customs and histories of the cultures we would encounter along the route. She, Maggie and Liza – the girls, I have to confess, reluctantly and sometimes grumpily – began tutorials in Swahili given by a member of my staff whose father, a Zairean, is a professor at the University of Dar es Salaam and whose mother is an African American. We posted a Michelin map of the region on the door leading to the pantry, just off our kitchen. On it, we traced our route in red ink.

I have to confess that I began to think what a mad idea it was to attempt to take one's family on a three-thousand-mile journey, over three weeks, though three African countries, accompanied virtually every minute by a six-person camera crew consisting of Britons. Could I take our family therapist along as well? I wondered. However, the BBC's agreement to give Sharon and our daughters the formal role I had requested enabled each of us to assume a new identity, almost like professional actors in a play, thereby diminishing the force of our roles as members of a family. Nothing proved to be more crucial to the success of our enterprise than this, I am convinced, especially since I arranged for part of my fee to be given to Maggie and Liza, and had the series producer send them a mock contract. 'It's a difficult job,' they were heard to say at the most trying of times during our trip, 'but a contract is a contract.'

The trip was glorious, despite the obvious hardships. I had two main aims in mind. First, I wanted my family to experience a variety of African cultures 'on the ground', as it were, and not on an expensive pampered 'safari' or out of the windows of Hilton hotels. I wanted Maggie and Liza to be able to determine for themselves just what they did – and did not – have in common with Africa and its Africans. Second, I wanted to return to the shadows of my own adolescence, to retrace in part my own steps a quarter of a century earlier, to go back to the tiny, isolated village where I had lived so far from all that was

ABOVE Near the village of Kilimatinde, Henry Louis Gates with (left to right),
his daughters Maggie and Liza, and his wife Sharon

OPPOSITE Despite appearances, the Indian Ocean port of Dar es Salaam in
Tanzania is now rough and down-at-heel

safe and familiar, surrounded by deeply devout Christians who were as passionate in their beliefs in God and in an afterlife as they were brutally, desperately poor.

Tanzania in 1970 was one of the twenty poorest countries in the world, and Kilimatinde lay in the centre of the most impoverished region of Tanzania. I wanted the girls – who live in a house surrounded by African art, and whose godfathers are a Nobel Prize-winning African writer and a Harvard African philosophy professor – to experience the lives of people whose annual earnings are far less than their allowances for Christmas gifts. I wanted them to see, from the ground, Africa's dense array of exotic plants and wildlife. And I wanted them, most of all, to encounter for themselves their own African American culture – especially our music and our cultural heroes – in the mouths and on the dance floors of the African cousins they never realized they had. I wanted them to learn that we were no longer Africans, and that we were, at the same time and inevitably, an African people in the New World, a satellite culture circling around a delightfully mysterious and vast continent of black customs, beliefs and cultures.

We decided to use as one of the trip's motifs the route that David Livingstone, my boyhood hero, had taken in his quest to find a trans-continental water route connecting the Indian Ocean to the Atlantic. To prepare the girls, who had never been to Africa before, we visited Soweto in South Africa, then spent a short holiday with friends in Namibia; the two venues represented Africa's extremes. Then we headed for Harare in Zimbabwe, where we met the BBC crew and began our voyage of discovery.

Our rail journey began early on the morning of 8 August. As the conductor said pointedly to me, 'Welcome, my brother,' I could not help but think of the fact that, at the time of my first visit twenty-five years earlier, South Africa, Namibia and Rhodesia (now Zimbabwe) had all been outposts of the white racist colonial system known as apartheid. Following what seemed like hours of being filmed boarding and disembarking from the train at Harare, we took the three-hour trip to the medieval ruins called Great Zimbabwe.

Here we met our guide, Prospero, before whose command of the history of this magnificent place I felt like Caliban. How complex this ancient civilization must have been, to construct this stunning monument of stone architecture as a testament to their sense of their own power, nobility and elegance as much as to stake a claim on beauty and well-guarded strength in a universe full of chaos that lay just beyond the borders of the castle's compound.

Constructed at the time of Europe's Middle Ages, Great Zimbabwe must be one of the seven wonders of the African world. Except for the medieval structures at Djena and Timbuktu in Mali, and Axum and Lalibela in Ethiopia, Great Zimbabwe is sub-Sahara's grandest architectural ruin – so grand, in fact, that British colonials decided it was much too sublime to have been created by black Africans and concocted the most bizarre theories – that it had been created by Phoenicians or Jewish traders, by Asians, by Arabs, even by northern Europeans. One wit decided it was more plausible to attribute its origins to extra-terrestrials than to black people! Europe seemed quite desperate to deny responsibility to the Zimbabweans themselves.

I thought of this irony as I stood on the 'King's Table' of the 'Acropolis' of the ruin's palace, from which successive kings could observe their twenty-odd thousand subjects as they tilled their land and tended their herds. This, the great black Athens, bore the most eloquent witness against the charges that persons of African descent, and their cultures, were inferior to those found in Europe or Asia or even in the New World. I wondered, too, as I stood high above this lovely valley, if I were the only black man in this world who felt like throwing a party every time one of the Leakeys discovered even another toe bone from our human antecedents. Not only was it on this great continent that the human community was born, but the ruins at Great Zimbabwe attested to the sublime artistic and metaphysical gifts of those very people – black people. Africa, these ruins proved, before it was ravaged by colonialism, comprised civilizations as subtle and as compelling as any to be encountered in Europe. Standing before the palatial temples and castles at Great Zimbabwe, suddenly I thought I understood how a European might feel standing before Chartres or Westminster Abbey for the very first time. So much has been lost in Europe's scramble for Africa, but little has been as devastating as the loss of the world's knowledge of African culture and history. While Maggie and Liza had already been astounded by the sort of poverty that

DFH₂060

ABOVE AND OPPOSITE Trains at the Tazara Station, Dar es Salaam,
terminus of the route from Zambia. The line was built in the 1970s to give
landlocked Zambia easier access to the sea

we had witnessed out of our train windows, nothing could interrupt their experience of the sheer beauty of Great Zimbabwe.

Our first game reserve, at Hwange, was most certainly one of the high points of our journey. We stayed at the Katchana camp, which had opened only one week before. We arrived very late on the evening of 11 August, having taken the train from Bulawayo to Dete. We arrived without our bags because Stanley, one of our two drivers, had boarded the train at one of our several stops in order to enjoy his lunch. And there he remained, merrily munching away on chicken and rice as the train made its way out of the station, further and further away from Stanley's Land Rover, full of the crew's equipment as well as most of our own baggage.

When we pulled into our destination, half the crew joined our family and off we headed for the game park. The others waited for Stanley (who had long since disembarked and, we hoped, made his way back to the Land Rover) and the driver of our second vehicle to surface. While we waited, somewhat exhausted by eagerness as well as anxiety, we explored Katchana.

We were the only guests. Jonathan, our host, was a Zimbabwean who had lived in the States. His brother David, a student in England, was visiting him as well. A white Zimbabwean driver called Debbie had ferried us from the station to the game park – uneventfully except for when she referred to the use of the bush as a toilet as 'piccaninny kayaks'. Piccaninny is a term of racist abuse in the States; I recall my astonishment that it was used so commonly in Britain when I was a postgraduate at Cambridge in the mid-seventies; I certainly was not prepared to hear it from the mouth of a white ex-Rhodesian. I had always had some difficulty accepting the concept of a 'white African'; Debbie's 'piccaninny kayak' remark forced me to wonder how much had changed in post-colonial Zimbabwe.

Our suites – built high on stilts – looked out over a small watering-hole, where early in the morning we could watch a remarkable variety of animals. When we heard an elephant trumpet, we discovered with as much excitement as trepidation that most game reserves were surrounded by an electric fence to keep out errant lions or elephants – but not ours. For warmth – it was bitterly cold, with the Southern Cross revealed as clear as a drawing in the blue-black icy crystal sky – we huddled at the bar, downing gin and tonic close to the warmth of two small bonfires blazing in sunken earthen circles, like natural circular hearths. (Liza ordered a gin, *straight*, after sneaking a sip of my gin and tonic!) A magnificent feast ensued, with beef and fish and loads of cauliflower and other vegetables, and a marvellous selection of South African wines. When Stanley, his mate and our bags finally arrived, hardly anyone noticed. Liza slept with the lights on, figuring that the elephant we had heard would be deterred by her night light just as it would by a campfire.

Early the next morning, we headed off 'to see the animals at last'. Our driver was a black Zimbabwean named Charles. Maggie, hawk-eye that she is, was the first to spot a giraffe, so majestic in its loping elegance. Zebra and impala strolled all over the place, as common as pigeons in Trafalgar Square. Charles was well trained and quite knowledgeable, especially about birds such as the lilac-crested roller. Because he had been programmed to deliver his pat lecture at set points in the game park and could not be deterred from his routine, we failed to come upon the herd of elephants we had been tracking all morning, following their droppings like Hansel and Gretel in the Black Forest. Maggie and Liza were tremendously frustrated, as were we all, especially Graham, our cameraman. Then Maggie spotted a young male, so delighted by all the attention we paid him that he seemed to be posing for the camera. One young male was as good as a herd!

After this treat we drove through a dry river bed, called a 'flay', passing what seemed like a Noah's Ark full of animals, before we arrived at a safari park called Sikumi Tree Lodge. It looked like the Hilton to us, replete with a swimming pool, manicured grounds and dramatic views of a wide variety of wildlife sipping away easily from a fairly substantial watering-hole. Here, following a lavish lunch we interviewed Lionel Reynolds, a fifth-generation white Zimbabwean, who was the manager of the lodge. Lionel, educated in England, is a sensitive man, most lovingly obsessed with elephants, 'the true king of the jungle,' he proclaimed. He invited us to 'walk up on an elephant', an invitation that Sharon and I eagerly accepted.

Driving to the spot in the bush from which we would set out on foot, we stumbled upon the very herd of elephants that had proved so elusive earlier that day. We sat in stunned silence at the grace of these mammoth grey hulks of wrinkled skin and ivory, foot pads larger than family-sized pizzas, almost bashfully flirting with their wide eyes. After they dispersed we climbed out of Lionel's Land Cruiser, desperately attempting to memorize his instructions as I watched, dumb-struck, while he loaded his elephant gun. 'Just a precaution,' he laughed.

Within minutes we were in a crouching position, close by Lionel and his gun, just fifteen metres from what looked to me like the Empire State Building on four feet with a trunk. But the elephant, apparently, was not amused by our presence, and began to stomp the earth and shake his head. 'He's threatening to charge us,' Lionel whispered, with a hint of surprise in his voice. 'Show some respect . . . mind your manners,' he shouted as he stood up defiantly, slapping his right palm against the butt of the rifle. To my enormous relief, the elephant did. 'You've got to treat them like you would a blustering adolescent,' Lionel whispered.

'Uh-huh,' I thought, 'just relax and enjoy the view.'

Well, while I was relaxing and enjoying the view – and, quite frankly, measuring the time and distance it would take for me to run back to our Land Cruiser — two more elephants approached us from Lionel's blind side. I began to tap Lionel on his right hip pocket; he had instructed us firmly not to utter a sound. 'Relax . . . relax,' he kept whispering. Finally he turned and directed his astonished gaze in the direction of my trembling index finger.

These two new, younger, elephants came close enough to form the left branch of a Y, with the first elephant comprising the right branch. The three of us formed the junction of the Y's three lines. The oldest elephant, whom Lionel said was about fifteen or sixteen, stomped the earth. Even we could smell our own fear. Lionel fronted him again, firmly and boldly, as the elephant decided whether or not to charge.

'Had he charged,' Lionel confessed to us after we had made our deliberate but hurried retreat to the vehicle, descending down the tail of the Y, 'I would have had to shoot him, unfortunately.'

'Say what?' I thought.

'Just as he lowered his head to stab us with his tusks. He does that at the last minute, just a few feet from his prey.'

A few *feet*? I wondered. Lionel would have confronted that elephant on his own.

An orange-seller plies his trade

As I have confessed, I have sometimes had difficulties with the notion of a white African, as I remembered when Debbie referred to 'piccaninny kayaks'. But just then, Lionel looked to me like the blackest man I knew. 'Lionel,' I said, 'you're the baddest African on the continent.' We laughed and drank and hugged, so relieved to be alive.

'Come back, brother,' he said at our departure. 'After all, it's your continent.' We drove on to Victoria Falls, wrapped in a warm and peaceful silence.

At Victoria Falls I experienced the sublime for the first time, I believe, in my life. Terror, beauty and awe: Niagara Falls seemed like a shower compared to this great passage of water. After meeting the impressive Shona sculptor Nicholas Mukomberanwa, who bears an uncanny resemblance to the African American painter Jacob Lawrence, we visited the great Victoria Falls Hotel, a vestige of the colonial era if ever there was one. The head porter, who reminded me of my Uncle Jim, told me of his great admiration for Jesse

Jackson and Randall Robinson. Of Colin Powell, a *New Yorker* profile of whom I was writing at night on our rail journey, he asked, 'Is there a brother under that uniform?' I was astonished at his knowledge of, and fascination with, African Americans, just as I was constantly surprised to hear Michael Jackson's voice booming out of station loudspeakers and transistor radios, and to see Mike Tyson's image used so often as a logo for makeshift barber shops.

All of the contradictions of colonialism are epitomized by Victoria Falls. Livingstone, widely reputed to have 'discovered' it, of course did nothing of the kind. He was taken to the Falls by friendly local Africans whose ancestors had long ago named it 'Mosi-oa-Tunya', which means 'the smoke that thunders'. Why Robert Mugabe and his compatriots had not changed its name at independence in 1980, when they rechristened Rhodesia Zimbabwe after the medieval ruins, remains a mystery to me. It was here that Livingstone conceived his great dream to bring 'Civilization, Commerce and Christianity' to the benighted Africans who had lived here for centuries, hoping, as he did, that what I think of as the three Cs of colonialism could transform the magnificent Zambezi River into a virtual highway for the European scramble to exploit Africa's natural wealth. Livingstone was an ardent abolitionist and inspired almost blind loyalty in his black servants. But his terrible legacy is a century of European domination of black people and their cultures which Europe devalued, maligned, mocked and often attempted to destroy. The huge statue of Livingstone on the Zimbabwe side of the Falls, placed there in 1955 by the white South African apartheid government and moulded in a neo-fascist style reminiscent of statues of Marx, Lenin and Stalin in the ex-Soviet Union, was intended to underscore the complete submission of black Africa to its white colonial heritage. It should be replaced, and the name of the Falls changed to its African original.

Early in the morning of 14 August we boarded a train for the one-hour journey to Livingstone, Zambia – a beautiful ride across the Falls. The short distance between the Zimbabwean side and the Zambian side belies the enormous differences between the two towns that exist there. The town of Victoria Falls in Zimbabwe remains something of a neo-colonial outpost in a proudly independent, post-apartheid, quasi-democratic state. Livingstone, on the other side, is not the tourist's favourite of the two: its Hotel Inter-Continental compares poorly with the grand, highly rated hotels of Victoria Falls. Relatively run down and slightly ramshackle, Livingstone is to Victoria Falls as the Third World is to the First. There was no need for advance reservations here.

After lunch we visited the traditional African village of Mukuni. It is ruled over by King Mukuni who lives in Lampasa Palace, a place of mud walls covered with photographs of his ancestors and coloured anthropological drawings of 'how our people once dressed', and roofed with thatch. This is the home of the Batoka-Leya people, and it has been their home for a thousand years. The King – 'chief', he advised me when I enquired, was a derogatory European coinage, meant to diminish the status of traditional African monarchs and simultaneously to elevate by contrast the status of the occupants of Windsor Castle – is a direct descendant of a millennium of fathers and grandfathers and their fathers and grandfathers.

This was just the sort of phenomenon that I wished my daughters to experience. King Mukuni had been educated at the University of Zambia, where he studied economics. For a brief period, while his father reigned, he worked for British Petroleum. He had visited Britain once, he is a devout Roman Catholic, and he is determined that his village will survive, despite its enormous poverty. 'Subsistence farming is our principal occupation,' he told me, 'but tourism has become our number one crop.' The King was quite proud of a certificate he'd received for bungee-jumping off the bridge over the Falls.

We were welcomed by traditional dancers, two of whom wore bones in their noses. Our audience with the King was preceded by a cleansing ritual in which a priestess 'sprayed' us with a sacred potion, spat on to our faces from her mouth. The girls sat crouched in a lotus position, quite astonished at this peculiar form of welcome! 'They welcome us by spitting in our faces,' Liza would relate to one of her friends back home. Our day at the village ended with the entire village singing 'The Noble Leya Anthem', a poignant lament for the loss of Mosi-oa-Tunya to Victorian Britain.

'Wouldn't you prefer to be enjoying the luxuries of the city?' I asked the King cautiously, as we were leaving.

OPPOSITE A small boy sells bananas
ABOVE Street hawkers in Dar es Salaam
In Africa, even the youngest contribute to the family economy

'I'm at the centre of a great civilization here, and I am content,' he replied.

I believed him, as I peered at the villagers' mud huts.

Mukuni village would contrast starkly with Kilimatinde in the heart of Tanzania. Slowly we made our way through Zambia, a poor but democratic nation of 8 million, after visiting the country's most symbolic monument, the graves of the members of the Zambian national football team who were tragically killed in a fatal plane crash in 1973.

We met Zambia's most famous football commentator, Dennis Liwewe, who was born in a mud hut in the eastern part of Zambia. As a schoolboy, Dennis had recited Shakespeare in the bush behind his school. He finished first in his class, with the encouragement of his New Zealand headmaster.

He described to us what happens when the country's President comes to a game. The President arrives half an hour before the game is due to begin, then drives round and round the great circle of the field while the crowd stands and cheers. Then Dennis appears and announces the starting line-up. After each name is called the crowd becomes even more delirious. 'How can I not believe in God?' Dennis asks me as we are leaving the stadium. 'I only missed the fated plane by ten minutes.'

The next day we visited Kenneth Kaunda's praise-singer, or *griot*, who had composed a praise-song in my honour. Words such as 'Harvard' and 'Cambridge' were instantly recognizable amidst a whirl of strange lyrics. He was a spirit medium, he told us; his spirit's voices come 'from the Congo'. He wore a leopardskin vest, and he and two other drummers played the *inshingili*, a trio of three drums; his was made in 1922, four years after he was born. His 'great ancestor', he continued, was a spirit from the Kola people in Zaire, and it spoke to him regularly, giving him messages to share with President Kaunda during his long presidency of the country. The praise-singer's dancing and chanting reminded me uncannily of the dances that black Americans perform when they are 'possessed by the Holy Ghost'. And like his people, African Americans traditionally attributed special mystical powers to the Congo – the old name for Zaire. Place Congo in New Orleans, for example, was one of the early sites where jazz was created and performed.

We were joined on this visit by Mapopa Mtonga, Professor of African Mythology at the University of Zambia. How fortunate he is to be so near to his subject, a living, breathing, dancing mythology unfolding before one's very eyes.

Afterwards we made our way to the station, then on to Kabwe, where we arrived at 2.30 in the morning, exhausted and starving. Poor Maggie stepped off the van that met our train in pitch darkness, right into a pothole, and sprained her ankle. It required emergency ice packs and bandages – not the easiest items to locate in the middle of Zambia.

On our trip to Kabwe I had interviewed Gladys Mutukwa, Zambia's leading feminist politician. She was preparing to attend the Women's Conference in Beijing two days later, and had joined us on the train late at night specially for our interview. What a breath of fresh air! 'Economically,' she confessed, 'things are worse today than they were twenty-five years ago. Down-sizing, urbanization . . . all these things.' In the face of such harsh economic realities few African intellectuals can afford the sort of romanticism indulged in by American 'Afrocentrists' in their attitudes to traditional and contemporary Africa. Many people think that Ms Mutukwa, the sole woman in her law school year and only the third woman in Zambian history to take a law degree, could be Zambia's first female head of state. After the economy, her biggest concern was the prevention of female genital mutilation. 'It is still prevalent,' she says, 'as are misogyny, violence against women, malnutrition and homelessness. All because of corruption, inefficiency and false starts such as socialism, which had a dehumanizing effect.' Reform is needed, she notes; drastic reform. Near Kabwe we bade each other farewell; we wished her well in Beijing.

By morning Maggie's ankle was a dull reddish purple, swollen to three times its usual size. Still, we filmed early that afternoon at 'The Old Slave Tree', a rest-stop on an Arab slave route that extended from the interior to Dar es Salaam. Before the shoot Stuart Murphy, our superb assistant producer, and I had gone to Cecil Rhodes' famous zinc mine and learned that Rhodes'

OVERLEAF **Between Bagamoyo and Kilimatinde, the train ahead of the Gates's crashed, and all aboard had to trans-ship**

agents had found zinc here in 1902, had formed the Broken Hill Development Company in 1904, and in 1906 had extended his railroad to Kabwe; it was on his line that Rhodes had finally visited the place. But this far and no more: at Kabwe, Rhodes' grand dream of a trans-continental railway ended. As I narrated later that afternoon:

> This is Kabwe, the end point of the Zambian Railroad, and the northern end point of Cecil Rhodes' attempt to colonize Africa from the Cape to Cairo.
>
> Rhodes founded the Broken Hill mine here, now defunct, to plunder its rich supply of zinc. And it was at this mine, ironically enough, that another discovery was made. Zambia's most famous archaeological remains, *Homo Rhodesiensis* – a human skull thought to be over seventy thousand years old – was discovered by a miner in 1921, helping to establish Africa as the site for the origin of the human species.
>
> The exploitation of Africa's minerals was not as lucrative as its exploitation in human beings. I am standing under a site named 'The Slave Tree'. Here, thousands and thousands of slaves – perhaps even one of my ancestors – were allowed a rest, perhaps some water, before they continued north, then east, to the great port at Dar es Salaam, hence to be shipped abroad. History has not even begun to record the suffering that was shared under the tree.
>
> If Cecil Rhodes hung back at Kabwe, David Livingstone, undeterred, pressed on, just as we shall press on, in search of Livingstone's legacy.

From Kabwe we drove to Kapiri Mposhi to catch a train on the famous Tazara railroad, built by the Chinese in the early 1970s to free landlocked Zambia from its dependence upon apartheid Rhodesia and South Africa for routes to the sea. Other nations had refused to participate in the construction of the Tazara, in order to keep Zambia dependent. The Chinese proceeded to do it themselves, sending in their own workforce and equipment, completing in record time a project that many had declared to be 'unfeasible'. This railroad, initially call the Tanzam and nicknamed the Uhuru railroad (*Uhuru* means 'freedom' in Swahili) was under construction when I lived here twenty-five years ago.

At Mbeya, Sharon, Liza and I spent hours climbing Lake Ngosi, a crater left by a crashing meteorite. Never have I been closer to what we think of as 'the jungle'; never were we in greater danger than on its narrow pathways, high above the surrounding terrain. The view of the lake, deep in the crater's bottom, was well worth the arduous climb: the Safwa people have spun a cycle of creative myths around this sacred place, to which they traditionally came on pilgrimage once a year to make sacrifices. They call the meteor's landing 'the day of rolling thunder'. Liza climbed up and down like a gazelle; Sharon and I like octogenarians! As we headed back to the hotel, exhausted, we passed a painting of Michael Jackson on the mud wall of a village store, with his song 'Why' booming out of nowhere. It occurred to me that I might be more exhausted than I realized, and that I had begun to hallucinate. But no: Michael Jackson was a star, even at Lake Ngosi.

We traversed my beloved Tanzania from its south-western border with Zambia all the way to the coast. I was impatient to see Dar again, to visit Oyster Bay, the site of the home of the USIS Director with whom I had lived for six weeks after bidding farewell to missionary life in Kilimatinde. Dar was so disappointing: a once clean and lovely city is somewhat ramshackle now, its beautifully sited harbour polluted by the direct dumping of raw sewage. Robberies are routine on the beaches, even the beaches across the road from Oyster Bay's great mansions. More than this, an air of defeat hangs over the city. Gone forever are the untested dreams of *Ujamaa*, the noble effort to change the nature of African human beings, or to return to some sort of *ur*-tribal self, called the 'African collective', under the direction and guidance of that philosopher-king from Edinburgh, Mwalimu Julius Nyerere, Tanzania's first and only president until he resigned two decades later. Not even this good and decent man could find that collective tribal self and build an economic order around it. He couldn't find it because it doesn't exist.

OVERLEAF **Village festivities to welcome Henry Louis Gates back to Kilimatinde**

From Dar we drove up the coast to Bagamoyo, from where Livingstone had set out in his attempt to discover the source of the Nile, through which Henry Morton Stanley had passed in his quest to find Livingstone, and to which Livingstone's two loyal servants had carried his pickled body so that it could be shipped back for burial in England. Bagamoyo was a centre of the slave trade, as well as a centre of the fight to abolish it. Slaves from the interior freed by the missionaries formed their own village here, where they were educated and lived out their lives, rather than returning to their homes. As a testament to the transforming power of their arduous, traumatic trek through the interior, no matter what their tribal identity had been they were now members of a new tribe, the Pan-African tribe of ex-slaves.

Our trip ended in Kilimatinde, after we had been delayed for eighteen hours when the train in front of us crashed on the single track line which took us inland from Bagamoyo. It was almost twenty-five years to the very day since I had first arrived there, in total shock at how different it all was and how very far from home I was. Now I was returning to this tiny world apart, surrounded and protected by my wife and our two daughters.

What had I hoped to find? I am not quite sure.

I certainly did not expect Maggie and Liza to bond mystically with their putative African heritage, with a past they never had. No, I think now, in retrospect, that I wanted to re-encounter the shadows of my own quest for clarification of my generation's relation to 'Africa', and I wanted to re-encounter that pivotal episode in my education wrapped in the protective armour of my family. Most of all, I was desperate to meet someone who knew me then, through whose eyes I could see myself then, at the age of nineteen.

An evil thing has happened to the village of Kilimatinde. The missionaries, with whom I fought so fiercely and so often about politics and their own racism towards the Africans in the village, were gone. Gone, too, were the funds that their churches had sent to maintain the hospital and the homes that formed the compound. A sleepy little village of five hundred was now, a quarter of a century later, a desperately impoverished village of ten thousand. AIDS is so prevalent that we were discouraged from visiting the hospital where I had delivered general anaesthesia for so many operations.

The entire village had declared a holiday in our honour. The bishop was in attendance, various dancing and singing groups competed to entertain us, and Maggie, Liza and Sharon made speeches in the church that I had been required by the missionaries to attend daily. Then we were all made members of the Wagogo tribe. I was moved to tears by my family's understanding of my need for a reunion, and their appreciation of the village's warmth at this return of a native son whom no one could even remember. (When Nick Shearman, our film's director, had walked into the church to prepare them for my arrival the entire congregation stood and applauded, assuming that *he* was their long-lost cousin!)

To my surprise and dismay, I found myself – despite myself – longing for the order and the resources that the missionaries had brought to the Wagogo in earlier years. Their residences, as well as the hospital buildings, were in great disrepair. The standard of living, and the villagers' life expectancy, had not been raised one jot over the past two decades. Looking around the village, I was forced to realize that even if the West stood still for a thousand years, my friends in Kilimatinde would never catch up. And the West, of course, will never stand still.

I thought of this as we drove our Land Rover down the badly pitted road that connects the fringe of the escarpment with the Great Rift Valley, seen through a reddish purple haze as the equatorial sun abruptly descended at seven, like a curtain on a school play. (Unlike Mukuni village, no crop of tourism promises to save Kilimatinde.) Four hours later we arrived at the capital city of Dodoma, covered with the dust of thirty miles after making our way slowly through the bush, away from this village where all the people are black.

So we had made our curious little pilgrimage: three weeks, three African countries, three thousand miles – and we had never needed our freephone family therapy number! Throughout our journey I had been plagued by my determination that our daughters should make this trip. Why had it been so very important to me? In Dar es Salaam I met a white American USIS official who had told me of her own concerns about her daughter's familiarity with her father's Indian culture. 'The most that you can hope for at your daughters' ages,' she had counselled me, 'is to plant the seeds.' And maybe, just maybe, that is enough.

Index

Index